Anglo-American Cataloging Rules

NORTH AMERICAN TEXT

Prepared by   The American Library Association
The Library of Congress
The Library Association and
The Canadian Library Association

CHAPTER

6

Separately Published Monographs

Incorporating chapter 9, "Photographic and Other Reproductions," and revised to accord with the

International Standard Bibliographic Description (Monographs)

American Library Association/Chicago 1974

Library of Congress Cataloging in Publication Data
Main entry under title:

Anglo-American cataloging rules.

   "The redrafting ... for this revision was undertaken
by Paul W. Winkler, Principal Descriptive Cataloger of
the Library of Congress."
   1. Descriptive cataloging. I. Winkler, Paul Walter,
ed. II. American Library Association. III. United
States. Library of Congress.
Z694.A48 1974   025.3'2   74-10946
ISBN 0-8389-3156-1

CONTENTS

Preface   v

Chapter 6.   1

Appendix I. Glossary: Additions and revisions   114

Appendix III. Abbreviations: Additions and

                                revisions   117

Appendix V. Punctuation and diacritics   118

Concordance of rule numbers   121

PREFACE

This revision of Chapter 6 of the Anglo-American Cataloging Rules, North American Text, was occasioned primarily by the desire of the authors to incorporate the provisions of the International Standard Bibliographical Description (Monographs)[1] into the text in regular cataloging rule form.   All changes in the rules agreed upon by the authors in the period since the original publication have also been incorporated. In addition those changes in Appendixes I, III, and V required by the revision of Chapter 6 have been included. Appendixes II, IV, and VI were not affected by the revision.

With respect to its provision for indicating authorship, rule 142E1 is to be regarded as provisional. The matter of authorship indication was not adequately explored in the formulation of the ISBD(M) and time constraints for preparation of copy for this revision of Chapter 6 prevented adequate discussion among the authors of the North American Text as to the best course to be followed under the

---

1. International Federation of Library Associations. ISBD(M), International Standard Bibliographical Description for Monographic Publications. 1st standard ed.   (London, IFLA Committee on Cataloguing, 1974)

circumstances. The present text, therefore, differs little in substance from the rule in the 1967 text.

The redrafting necessary for this revision was undertaken by Paul W. Winkler, Principal Descriptive Cataloger of the Library of Congress. The following members of the Library's Descriptive Cataloging Division have been responsible for preparation of camera-ready copy for the publication: Lucille Johnson typed the copy; Betty C. Donohue, Albert G. Kohlmeier, and Elena Stanka did the proofreading.

SEPARATELY PUBLISHED
MONOGRAPHS

Introductory Notes

Purpose. The purpose of cataloging a separately published monograph is to identify it and to distinguish it from other
works and also from other editions of the same work and, in
some instances, from other issues of the same edition. The
description may also require that the nature and scope and
the bibliographical history and relationships of the work be
explained.

Identification. To distinguish one work from another,
the title (together with the author's name as heading) is generally sufficient; for anonymous and pseudonymous works,
other details, such as the statement which veils rather than
names the author, or the imprint, are necessary in order
to distinguish two works with the same title.

To distinguish one edition from another of the same work,
one or more of the following must be known: number or name
of the edition, name of the editor, illustrator, translator, or
publisher, date of publication,[1] name of the series to which

---

1. A work that has a different copyright date is assumed
to be a different edition even though all other elements of the
description are the same.

the edition belongs, or some detail of physical description such as the number of pages or volumes in the work. Since the user of the catalog rarely knows all of these details about the work he is seeking, and since in a growing library it cannot be foreseen which of them will be necessary to distinguish the various editions to be acquired, it is essential to include in each catalog entry all pertinent information of this type (see 134-142). To distinguish the various issues of a given edition, any of a wide variety of details may need to be specified.[2]

Description. The elements in the catalog entry that identify the work and distinguish it from other works and other editions of the same work frequently supply all of the descriptive data that are necessary. Additional data may be necessary, however, to amplify or explain a title which is inadequate or misleading as to the nature or scope of the work, or to explain the bibliographical history and relationships of the work (see 143).

---

2. It is not the policy of the Library of Congress, except in certain cases of rare books, to collect the various issues of a given edition and consequently no attempt is made to describe works in detail sufficient to identify them as issues. Various issues are added to the collection as copies if the description of the first one cataloged fits those received later in all details except the imprint date or the form of the publisher's name or both. Issues that vary only in place of publication or place of publication and imprint date are generally treated as issues (see 152B). If there are other differences, the issues are generally treated as different editions.

GENERAL RULES

130. Organization of the description

A. The descriptive elements of the catalog entry consist of the following areas: 1) the title and statement of authorship area which consists of a) the title proper, b) parallel titles, other titles and other title information, and c) statements of authorship, including subsidiary authorship, e. g. names of editors, translators, writers of prefaces, and persons who prepared a work entered under a corporate body or a form heading (see 134); 2) the edition area which consists of a) the edition statement and b) statements of authorship relating to the particular edition (see 135); 3) the imprint area (see 136-140); 4) the collation area (see 141); 5) the series area (see 142); 6) the notes area (143-148); and 7) the ISBN area (see 149).[3]

---

3. It is the practice of the Library of Congress to present the descriptive elements of the catalog entry in a series of paragraphs. The first paragraph consists of areas 1-3. In Library of Congress terminology it is called "the body of the entry." However, in the case of works entered under title the body of the entry is presented in the form of a "hanging indention," the first line of the body of the entry occupying the position of the heading unless a uniform title is required. In that case the uniform title is presented as a heading, the body of the entry taking the form of a paragraph. The second paragraph consists of the collation and series areas. Notes are presented in as many succeeding paragraphs as necessary followed in a separate paragraph by the statement of the ISBN, binding, and price. In the case of works whose titles are in non-Roman scripts, a romanization of the title is provided (see 150). If the work is entered under a personal or corporate author the

B. The following elements may also be presented between the author statement and the imprint, if they are needed (e. g. for the identification of the work or to explain an added entry), if they are taken from the work itself, and if they can be stated succinctly: illustration statement (see 135F), number of volumes (135G).

131. Punctuation

Each area of the catalog entry is separated from the following area by a period-space-dash-space[4] (. --) unless the following area begins a new paragraph. In that case the preceding area ends with a period unless another punctuation mark, e. g. a closing bracket or parenthesis, makes the period unnecessary. The individual elements of an area are identified by prescribed punctuation, the details of which are given in the appropriate rule. With the exception of the period (.) and the comma (,) prescribed punctuation separating elements of the description is preceded and followed by a space; the period and the comma are only followed by a

---

romanization is interposed in parentheses on the line between the heading and the transcription of the title page title unless a uniform title is required. In that case the romanization is given in the lower right corner of the entry following the tracing. This practice is also followed for works having a uniform title as a heading. If the work is entered under title, in hanging indention form, the romanization is recorded in parentheses on the line above, beginning at the same indention as the title page title.

4. In typescript the dash is normally represented by two hyphens.

space. The following is a schematic illustration of the application of punctuation symbols:

> Title proper = parallel title : other title / statement of authorship. -- Edition statement / statement of authorship relating to the edition. -- Place of publication : publisher, date (place of printing : printer)
>
> number of volumes and/or number of pages : illustration statement ; size & accompanying materials. -- (Series ; numbering within the series : subseries ; numbering within the subseries ISSN)
>
> Notes.
> ISBN.

Colons, equal signs, or slashes appearing in the source of the description in a position other than that prescribed above for their use in cataloging may be retained in those cases in which they may be written without a space on either side. The spaces appearing in the source of the description are omitted in the catalog entry.

> Introduction to PL/I programming for library and information service /
> 2x2=8 : the story of a group of young men in the Soviet Zone of Germany /

When it is typographically impossible to omit spaces before and after these punctuation marks, another mark must be substituted for the one on the publication.

> Title page: Service to Children in Their Own Homes:
>   Its Nature and Outcome
> Transcription: Service to children in their own
>   homes, its nature and outcome /

<u>Title page:</u>   The
Conquistador in
California:
1535
The Voyage of Fernando Córtes to
Baja California in Chronicles
and Documents

<u>Transcription:</u> The conquistador in California, 1535 :
the voyage of Fernando Cortés to Baja California in chronicles and documents /

Punctuation marks other than the prescribed ones may be used as necessary and are given with normal spacing. However, prescribed punctuation must also be used even though double punctuation results. (See also Appendix V.)

Quo vadis? : A narrative from the time of Nero /
In the examples in this chapter which illustrate only a portion of a catalog entry, the punctuation appropriate to the next probable element is generally provided at the end of each example.

132. Source of description

A. In general, the series statement and the items which precede the collation represent the information presented by the work itself. The collation is the cataloger's description of the physical work and is limited to standard bibliographical terminology. The rest of the description may consist of statements quoted from the work or from other bibliographic sources, of statements phrased by the cataloger, or of a combination of the two if this results in the clearest and most concise statement.

B. For the following areas of the catalog entry, the primary sources of information are prescribed and listed in the preferred order of use:

Area	Primary source of information
Title and statement of authorship	Title page, or if there is no title page, the source from within the publication that is used as its substitute (see 133B1)
Edition statement and statement of authorship relating to the edition	Title page, preliminaries, and colophon
Imprint	Title page, preliminaries, and colophon
Series statement	Series title page, title page, half title, cover, anywhere else in the publication
ISBN	Anywhere in the publication or in data supplied by the publisher and accompanying the book

If the information is not available in a primary source, it is supplied from another source and is enclosed in brackets. One pair of brackets is used for adjacent interpolated elements that are within the same area. When adjacent interpolated elements are components of different areas, a separate pair of brackets to enclose the elements in each area is required. Prescribed punctuation is given outside the brackets.

[London : Midgely, 1973]
[1. ed.]. -- [Paris] : Desclée , De Brouwer, [1973]

133. Relationship of the title page to the description of a work

A. General rules

1. The title page together with data from other primary sources (see 132B) serves as the basis of the description to be presented in the areas that precede the collation. If an element prescribed for inclusion (see 130) is supplied from a source other than the title page or other primary source it is enclosed within brackets. If the elements normally on the title page are given on two facing pages or on successive pages or leaves, without repetition, the information is transcribed as if from one page without the use of brackets. If, however, the two pages represent a multi-volume work and one of its volumes, respectively, they are considered to be two title pages even if there is no repetition. If a letter or a word appears only once, but the title page design makes it clear that the letter is intended to appear in one or more other words, or that the word is to be repeated, the repetition is recorded without the use of brackets.

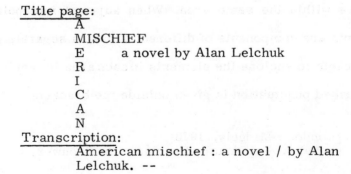

Title page:
```
        A
MISCHIEF
E       a novel by Alan Lelchuk
R
I
C
A
N
```
Transcription:
American mischief : a novel / by Alan Lelchuk. --

Title page:
>Canadian BIBLIOGRAPHIES canadiennes

Transcription:
>Canadian bibliographies = Bibliographies canadiennes /

Additions are given in the language or the script of the title page or of the particular element on the title page, except that the abbreviations "etc.," "i.e.," and "et al." are used in all languages and scripts. If an addition is conjectural, it is so indicated by a question mark.

>[Dublin? N. H.]
>Dublin [N. H. ?]

Descriptive information appearing on the title page which cannot be regarded as other title information (see 134C4c) should be quoted or given in a note phrased by the cataloger if it provides an essential amplification or qualification of the formal description.

2. If a statement that is transcribed from the title page or other primary source is inaccurate, it is recorded as it appears, followed (within brackets) either by the word "sic" for an obvious error or by the abbreviation "i.e." and the correction. Correction may also be made by supplying a missing letter or letters if only a single set of brackets is needed.

>Holy ghosts : pomes [sic] /
>The Paul Anthony Buck [i.e. Brick] lectures /
>What your child really wants to know about sex, and why / by Will[i]am A. Block. --

3. If case endings would be affected, or if the grammatical

construction of the title page data would be disturbed, a statement appearing on the title page is not transposed to observe the prescribed sequence (see 130) nor, in such cases, is a statement supplied from elsewhere in the work. Instead the sequence of statements on the title page is followed or the data are presented in a supplementary note.

4. If there are parallel titles or if the subtitle appears in several languages or scripts, the number of languages or scripts to be recorded is determined according to the provisions of 134C1. If other elements appear in several languages or scripts, only that element in the language or script of the title proper is transcribed (see also 138B4 and 142A1).

5. If the work does not have a title page to serve as the basis of the description, it is necessary to specify that a substitute has been used, unless the information has obviously been supplied by the cataloger (see 133B). If there are several title pages, one must be selected for use (see 133C).

B. Works without title pages

1. A work that is published without a title page, or without a title page applying to the whole work (as is the case of some editions of the Bible or of many bilingual dictionaries), is cataloged from some other part of the work if possible and that part specified as the source of the data (see 143D3a). The part of the work supplying the most complete information

is used as the substitute,[5] whether this be cover title, half title, caption title, colophon, running title, or other part. Additions and omissions are indicated and transpositions made in the same manner as when the title page itself serves as the basis of the description.

2. If no part of the work supplies data that can be used as the basis of the description, the necessary information is taken from any available source, whether this be a reference work (which is preferable) or the content of the work itself. This is necessary for works the title pages of which are lost, collections of pamphlets or other minor material assembled by the library or by a previous owner and which are to be cataloged as a single item, special numbers of periodicals without special titles which are to be cataloged as independent items, etc. (See also 134B5). Reprints of the several portions of a doctoral dissertation which together are considered by the university to which they were submitted as representing the published thesis, are cataloged as a single item under the title of the original thesis. In all such cases a single pair of brackets encloses the data from the title proper through the imprint.

C. Works with several title pages

1. A monographic work in several volumes is, as a rule,

---

5. Hereafter in the rules in this chapter, the term "title page" is used to include any substitute.

cataloged from the title page of the first volume. Variations
on the title pages of subsequent volumes are shown by incorporating the data with those from the first volume or by adding
supplementary notes.

> The first [-second] canto of the Lusiad.
> Vol. 2 has subtitle: Statistics of housing.

2. A one-volume work with more than one title page is
cataloged from the one that is most appropriate judged by the
following considerations:

a. The first title page is preferred unless the following
paragraphs give reason for choosing another.

b. If two title pages face each other, the second, which
occupies the customary position of the title page, is preferred,
unless one of the criteria in c-k below applies.

c. The title page bearing a later imprint date is preferred.

d. In the case of facsimile editions and reprint editions,
if there are both a new title page and a reproduction of the
original title page, the new title page is preferred.

e. A printed title page is preferred to an engraved one
since the latter may be used for various editions or issues
of the work.

f. If the title pages present the work in different aspects
(for example, as an individual work and as one volume of the
author's complete works) the one which corresponds with the

aspect in which the work is to be treated is chosen.

g. If there are title pages in more than one language or script, and text in but one language or script, the title page which is in the language or script of the text is preferred, unless the work is a text designed for students of a foreign language.

h. If there are title pages and text in more than one language, a title page that is in the original language of the work is preferred, unless a translation is known to be the reason for the publication, the original text being merely accessory to the translation.

j. If a bilingual dictionary has title pages in each of the languages, facing each other, preference is given to the title in the language of the readers for whom the dictionary appears to be intended, judging by the place of publication, the language of the prefatory matter, the language of abbreviations used, and the language of the second of the title pages.

k. Other things being equal, a title page is selected on the basis of language in the following order of preference: English, French, German, Spanish, Latin, any other language using the Roman alphabet, Greek, Russian, any other language using the Cyrillic alphabet, Hebrew, any other language using the Hebrew alphabet, any other language.

134. Title and statement of authorship area

    A. Punctuation

    1. The title proper is separated

    a. from the edition statement or the imprint by a period-space-dash-space (. --)

    b. from the statement of authorship by a space-slash-space (/)

    c. from a parallel title by a space-equal sign-space (=)

    d. from other titles or other title information by a space-colon-space (:)

(For punctuation of title page transcriptions of works without a collective title see 134C6)

    2. Other titles and other title information are separated

    a. from the edition statement or the imprint by a period-space-dash-space (. --)

    b. from the statement of authorship by a space-slash-space (/)

    c. from each other by a space-colon-space (:)

    3. Parallel titles are separated

    a. from the edition statement or the imprint by a period-space-dash-space (. --)

    b. from the statement of authorship by a space-slash-space (/)

    c. from other titles or other title information by a space-colon-space (:)

d. from each other by a space-equal sign-space (=)

4. The statement of authorship is separated from the edition statement or the imprint by a period-space-dash-space (. --). (For punctuation of multiple author statements see 134D5).

Examples of punctuation of the title and statement of authorship area:

> Title proper = parallel title = parallel title / statement of authorship. --
> Title proper : other title = parallel title : other title / statement of authorship. --
> Title proper : other title / statement of authorship. --
> Title proper / statement of authorship. --
> Title proper. --

B. Transcription of the title proper

1. General rule. The title proper (see also 134C) is transcribed exactly as to order, wording, spelling, accentuation, and other diacritical marks (if possible), but not necessarily as to punctuation and capitalization. If accents, umlauts, and other diacritical marks are omitted from the title page, they are added in conformity with the usage in the text. Typographic peculiarities, e.g. the use of v for u and i for j, are disregarded in works printed after 1500. An e above a vowel in German words is replaced by an umlaut. Chinese characters considered archaic, decorative, etc., are represented by the corresponding forms found in the K ang hsi tzŭ tien or Ueda's Daijiten, if possible, but simplified characters are transcribed as such. Symbols and

other matter that cannot be reproduced by the typographic facilities available are replaced by the cataloger's description.

> The factorial function [Illustration of the symbol chosen to stand for factorial base] ...

Line endings are indicated by two slashes without spaces to show that the title of a work is printed in verse or to distinguish two editions or issues of a rare book but only if all other methods are inadequate.

2. Abridgment. Long titles are abridged if this can be done without loss of essential information. The first words of the title are always included. Parts of the title more intelligibly presented in a contents paragraph are omitted from the transcription of the title (see 134C5). All omissions from the title are indicated by the mark of omission (...).

3. Author's name in title. If the title proper includes the statement of authorship, the name of the publisher, etc. and for linguistic or other reasons the statement must be regarded as an integral part of the title proper, it is so transcribed.[6]

> Marlowe's Plays
> Goethes Stücke
> Publii Ovidii Nasonis Fastorum libri sex
> The complete works of Charles Dickens

---

6. The same treatment is accorded author's names appearing in parallel titles, in other titles, or in other title information.

> Eileen Ford's A more beautiful you in 21 days
> Plato the teacher
> (Selections from Plato's works)
> Larousse's French-English dictionary, English-
> French dictionary
> Révai nagy lexikona
> Poesías del Sr. Dr. don Manuel Carpio con su
> biografía

If the publication has no title other than the name of the author, it is given as the title proper (see also 4 below).

> Longfellow
> Conference on Industrial Development in the Arab
> Countries.

4. Additions.

a. Additions may be made to the title in the language of the title if it needs explanation and if brief statements to clarify it can be taken from the work itself.

> Longfellow : [selections]. --
> Conference on Industrial Development in the Arab
> Countries : [proceedings]. --
> Mummer's fool : [poem]. --

b. When a title in a foreign language using the Roman alphabet begins with a numeral or an abbreviation (other than an initial of a personal name or an acronym), or contains a numeral or abbreviation that affects the filing, the corresponding word is supplied. In supplying words for numerals the accepted usage of the language is followed, e.g. in German "Hundert" not "Ein hundert." This is unnecessary, however, if both the abbreviation and the full form of the word it represents are the same as in English.

> 3 x [i.e. Dreimal] durch den Zaun

100 [i. e. Honderd] jaar spoorwegen in Nederland
1842 [i. e. Mil ochocientos cuarenta y dos] : panorama
y significación del movimiento literario
Dr. [i. e. Doktor] Sorge funkt aus Tokyo
Dr. -Ing. [i. e. Doktor-Ingenieur] Fritz Todt, 4. Sep-
tember 1891-8. Februar 1942
R. [i. e. Regia] Galleria di Firenze illustrata

Titles in other scripts do not need the amplification because the word is substituted for the numeral or abbreviation in the romanization of the title (see 150).

5. Supplied titles. If a title cannot be supplied from a reference source as provided in 133B2, one must be composed by the cataloger. In that case the nature and scope of the contents of the work are described in English as briefly as intelligibility permits.

C. Transcription of parallel titles, other titles and other title information

1. Parallel titles

a. If the title page has no more than two parallel titles both are recorded, with the exception noted in c below when one of the titles is in Chinese, Japanese, or Korean characters.

b. If there are more than two parallel titles the first is recorded unless c below is applicable. If one of the succeeding titles is in English it is also recorded. If the first title is written in a non-Roman script and there is no succeeding title in English, a title written in the Roman alphabet is also recorded, selected according to the following order of preference: French, German, Spanish, Latin, any other language using the Roman alphabet.[7]

c. If one of the titles is in Chinese, Japanese, or Korean characters, however, the language of the text takes precedence over the order of titles. If the text is unilingual the title matching that language is recorded. If the text is multi-lingual:

1) The title matching the language of the predominant text is recorded.

2) If there is no predominant text (e. g. a work with parallel text) the first title is recorded, provided there is matching text. If there is no matching text, the first title for which there is such a text is recorded.

3) If there is neither predominant text nor first title (as in a bilingual work with a horizontal title in Roman letters and a vertical title in characters), the title in the language dominant in the place of publication is recorded.

2. Original titles. If the original title appears on the title page of an edition of a work published with a different title, the original title is transcribed as a parallel title (see also 143D2)

> Die Geschichte von Frau Tiggywinkle = The story of Mrs. Tiggywinkle / von Beatrix Potter. --
> Love = L'envers de l'histoire contemporaine : a novel / from the French of Honoré de Balzac. --

---

7. National cataloging agencies record all parallel titles in the case of publications of the home country.

    Principles of survey analysis = formerly titled
Delinquency research / Travis Hirschi, Hanan C.
Selvin. --

3. Titles in romanization. If the title page of a work in a language using a non-Roman script includes also a romanized title, both titles are transcribed, separated by a space -equal sign-space (=).

4. Other titles and other title information. Other titles and other title information are transcribed in the order indicated by the sequence on, or the typography of, the title page. Other titles preceding the title proper on the title page are transposed to their proper position if grammatically possible. Otherwise they are given in a note (see 143D3b). Care must be taken not to interpret a series statement or other data at the head of the title as falling in the category of other titles and title information.

a. Alternative title. An alternative title is always transcribed in the catalog entry because the book may be referred to by it and because another edition may be published with the alternative title as the title proper.

b. Subtitle. The subtitle is transcribed in the entry in the same manner as the title proper, except that a long subtitle which is separable from the title proper may be omitted and quoted in a supplementary note, if this increases the clarity of the entry. A subtitle preceding the title proper on the title page, or appearing elsewhere in the publication, is transposed to the position determined by the general pattern of the catalog entry.

c. Other title information. Phrases on the title page which cannot be regarded as a subtitle or as an alternative title, but which are indicative of the character or general content of the work or of the motive for, or the occasion of, its publication are transcribed following parallel and other titles.

> Social work personnel for mental health programs : report of a conference held under the Southern Regional Program in Mental Health Training and Research, March 21-22, 1956, Atlanta, Georgia. --
> Horror man : the life of Boris Karloff : with an appendix of the films in which he appeared /
> Festschrift Ernst Kyriss : dem Bucheinbandforscher Dr. Ernst Kyriss in Stuttgart-Bad Cannstatt, zu seinem 80. Geburtstag am 2. Juni 1961 gewidmet von seinen Freunden. --

5. Works with both a collective title and titles of the individual works mentioned on the title page. If the title page bears a collective title and also the titles of the individual works contained in the publication, the titles of the individual works are given in a contents note (see 148).

> Three plays / by John Arden ; introduced by John Russell Taylor. --

> CONTENTS: The waters of Babylon. --Live like pigs. --The happy haven.

6. Works lacking a collective title. If a work lacks a collective title, and the title page bears only the titles of the individual works contained in it, the individual titles are transcribed in the order indicated by the sequence on, or

the typography of, the title page, a space - semicolon-space following each unless the titles are connected by a linking word or phrase. If these titles are accompanied by other titles of their own and/or statements of authorship, such other titles and statements of authorship are transcribed following the titles to which they are related. In this case each individual title with its accompanying elements is followed by a period (.) unless connected by a linking word or phrase.

Romeo and Juliet ; King Lear ; Macbeth / by William Shakespeare. --
Flash and filigree and The magic Christian / by Terry Southern. --
Henry Esmond : a novel / by Thackeray. Bleak House : a novel / by Charles Dickens. --

D. Statement of authorship

Preliminary note. The statement of authorship includes, in addition to the names of the authors, personal or corporate, the statement of the names of subsidiary authors, e.g. editors, translators, writers of prefaces, illustrators. (For the treatment of subsidiary authors related to the edition in hand, but not to all editions of a work, see 135D).

1.[8] Formal statements of authorship appearing in the work are given in the terms in which they are presented on the title page or elsewhere in the publication. If the statement of authorship does not follow the title elements on the

---

8. Alternative rule:
134D1. The statement of the name of the author may be omitted 1) unless the form of name in the heading is not

title page, it is transposed to the required position (see 130).
Author statements taken from a source other than the title
page but from within the publication are given in the prescribed position, enclosed in brackets. Statements taken from a
source outside the publication are recorded in a note if required
(see 143D3c). Statements of subsidiary authorship not appearing on the title page, in the preliminaries, or in the colophon
are recorded only if they are of special significance. If a
word or phrase occurring in conjunction with a statement of
authorship is indicative of the author's function rather than
of the content of the publication, it is treated as part of the
statement of authorship.

> Twentieth century plays / edited by Frank W. Chandler
> and Richard A. Cordell. --
> Scott's Ivanhoe / modernized and abridged by Carolyn
> Pulsifer Timm

but

> Underwater acoustics : a report / by the National

recognizably the same as that in the book, 2) unless there are
joint authors, collaborators, or contributors named in the
statement of authorship (see 134D5), 3) unless the name is
required to show the relationship of the work to the person
or corporate body named in the heading, or 4) unless the
name is an integral part of the title (see 134B3). Statements
of authorship which are recorded are given in the terms in
which they are formally presented on the title page or elsewhere in the publication. If the statement of authorship does
not follow the title elements on the title page, it is transposed to the required position (see 130). Author statements
taken from a source other than the title page but from within
the publication are given in the prescribed position, enclosed
in brackets. Statements taken from a source outside the
publication are recorded in a note if required (see 143D3c).

Environment Research Council Working Group. --

Statements which would be considered statements of authorship if a person or body were named are transcribed as
statements of authorship if they are significant, e. g. "Translated from the Swedish. "

2. If the title page bears an author statement in more than
one language, the statement that is in the language of the
title proper is given following the last recorded title element.

> Scientific policy, research, and development in Canada :
> a bibliography = La politique des sciences, la recherche
> et le developpment au Canada : bibliographie / prepared
> by the National Science Library. --
> Stein am Rhein (Schaffhausen) = Stein sur le Rhin
> (Schaffhouse) / [Ernst Rippmann ; adaptation française de
> Michelle Bouvier et Émile Villard]. --
>
> ("Adaptation" statement appears only in French)

3. When an author's name is an integral part of the title,
or is the title (see 134B3), no further author statement is
required.

4. When the name of a personal author or the name of a
corporate body has no grammatical relation to the title elements, the name is given immediately following the space-
slash-space (/) which separates the statement of authorship
from preceding elements.

> Le Père Goriot / Honoré de Balzac. --
> Handbook to the collections / Croydon Museum. --

5. When several authors including subsidiary authors are
recorded, the order is that indicated by the sequence on, or

the typography of, the title page. Names of several persons performing the same function in relation to the work are separated by commas; names of persons performing different functions are separated by a space-semicolon-space even though joined by linking words.

America yesterday / by Roy F. Nichols, William C. Bagley, and Charles A. Beard ; with drawings by George M. Richards
The Edwardian era / by André Maurois ; translated by Hamish Miles. --

6. Statements relating to supplementary material, e.g. bibliographies, appendices, which include the name of the person or corporate body preparing the material are transcribed as statements of authorship if found on the title page and follow those statements of authorship which relate to the work as a whole. For the treatment of supplementary material relating to the edition in hand but not to all editions of the work see 135D.

The spirited life : Bertha Mahony Miller and children's books / by Eulalie Steinmetz Ross ; selected bibliography compiled by Virginia Haviland. --

7. If there are more than three authors or more than three subsidiary authors performing the same function in the author statement, all after the first named are omitted. The omission is indicated by the mark of omission (...) and the phrase "et al.," the latter enclosed in brackets.

Background to archaeolgy : Britain in its European setting / Desmond Collins ... [et al.]. --

Animal motivation : experimental studies on the albino rat / by C. J. Warden ; with the collaboration of T. N. Jenkins ... [et al.]. --

8. Omissions from the author statement[9]

a. Titles and abbreviations of titles of address, honor, and distinction (but not of nobility), initials of societies, etc., are generally omitted from the author statement. Exception is made as follows:

1) If the title is necessary grammatically.

Prologo del Excmo. Sr. D. Manuel Fraga Iribarne. --

2) If the omission of the title leaves only the author's surname.

By Dr. Johnson. --

3) If the title is necessary for the identification of the author.

By Mrs. Charles H. Gibson. --

4) If the title explains the relationship of a personal author to the corporate author used as the heading for the work.

By Luther H. Evans, Librarian of Congress. --

b. For Chinese, Japanese, and Korean works in which the author statement contains a form corresponding to the name chosen for entry, any additional names or name forms are omitted, unless such omission would result in a distorted

---

9. Similar omissions are made from statements of editors, illustrators, translators, etc., appearing anywhere in the entry.

order of names.

9. Additions to the author statement

a. If necessary for intelligibility, a word or phrase in the language of the title is added in the case of a statement of personal authorship to express what is shown on the title page by arrangement, or to clarify an ambiguous or misleading statement, except that a preposition is not added to connect the author's name to the title elements (see 134D4) nor is a conjunction added before the last name if two or three names are recorded.

> The great ideas of Plato / [selected by] Eugene Freeman and David Appel. --
> Wolfram von Eschenbach : [Werke / hrsg.] von Karl Lachmann. --
> Antologija hrvatske poezije dvadesetog stoljeća od Kranjčevića do danas / [sastavili] Slavko Mihalić, Josip Pupačić, Antun Šoljan. --
> L'aviation / Paul Painlevé, Émile Borel. --

b. If it is not apparent that the name in a personal author statement refers to the same person as that represented by the main entry heading, the name in the heading, preceded by the abbreviation "i.e.," is added in brackets after the name in the author statement in direct form and with forenames abbreviated to initials.

> By Anthony Morton [i.e. J. Creasey]. --
> Heading: Creasey, John.

c. If the form of the name of a Chinese, Japanese, or Korean author, personal or corporate, chosen for entry, does not correspond to the form in the author statement, the characters for the entry form are added in the author statement.

Ono, Minemori, d. 830.
梅花引 ₍小₎野岑守作

Shu, Ch'ing-ch'un, 1898-
駱駝祥子　老舎₍舒慶春₎撰

135. Edition area

A. An edition statement in a work and any statements of authorship relating only to the particular edition of the work are always included in the catalog entry.   Statements relating to the impression or printing are included only in the case of items having particular bibliographical importance or when the impression or printing has been corrected or otherwise revised.   This makes it necessary for the cataloger to be aware of the lack of uniformity among publishers in the use of the terms "edition" and " impression" or "printing" and their equivalents in other languages, and to interpret them according to the accepted definitions.   In case of doubt as to whether the terms "edition," "edizione," etc., refer to an edition or to an issue of a work, the statement is given in its customary position, following the title or author statement.

B.   Punctuation

1.   The edition statement is separated

a.   from the imprint by a period-space-dash-space (. --)

b. from statements of authorship relating only to the particular edition by a space-slash-space (/) (For punctuation of multiple author statements see 134D5)

2. Any statements of authorship relating only to the particular edition are separated from the imprint by a period -space-dash-space (. --)

Examples of punctuation of the edition area:

> Edition statement / statement of authorship. --
> Edition statement. --

C. The edition statement is recorded as found in the work except that abbreviations are used (cf. Appendix III) and ordinal numerals are given in a standardized form (cf. Appendix IV H). If the edition statement, or any part of it, is taken from a source other than the title page, preliminaries, or the colophon it is enclosed in brackets.

> 2d ed. --
> New ed., rev. and enl. --
> 1st American ed. --
> Household ed. --
> 2. tirage revu et corrigé. --
> Reprinted March 1933 with corrections. --
> 3d ed., new impression. --
>   (Has new copyright date)

If a publication bears edition statements or statements of authorship relating to the edition in more than one language or script, only the statements in the language or script of the title proper are recorded. If a title page bears the titles of two or more works contained in the publication and one or more of these titles has its own edition statements, these statements are recorded in the title and authorship area following the title or the title and statement of authorship to which they apply.   Conventional punctuation is substituted for the prescribed punctuation in the edition area.

D. The edition statement is followed by a statement of any authors relating to the edition in hand, but not to all editions of the work.   Such authors include the reviser, the illustrator, and the writer of the preface of the particular edition.   If there is doubt that an author is related only to some editions of the work, the statement is recorded as part of the authorship statement of the work.   The names of authors relating to the edition are transcribed according to the provisions of 134D.

> 2d ed. / prepared with the assistance of M. E. Wise. --

E. If the volumes in a set are of different editions, the statement of the various editions is specified in a supplementary note or in the list of contents.

> On cover, v. 1: 3. éd. ; v. 2: 2. éd.
> CONTENTS: 1. deel. Klankleer, woordvorming, aard en verbuiging der woorden. 4. uitg. 1871. --2. deel. Leer van den volzin (syntaxis). 2. uitg. 1863. -- 3. deel. Stiljlleer. (Rhetorica, letterkundige encyclopaedie en kritiek) 2. verm. uitg. 1880.

A set containing volumes of various editions may also contain more than one edition of a given volume. In such case a note should call attention to this fact.

> Includes various editions of some volumes.
> Vol. 9, 3d ed. (1926) and 6th ed. (1950)

F. Illustration statement. A statement of illustrative matter appearing in the work that also includes the name of the artist is given if it appears on the title page, in the preliminaries, or in the colophon. The statement is treated as a statement of subsidiary authorship (see 134D) and is bracketed if it does not appear on the title page. If, however, it relates to the edition in hand but not to all editions of the work it is given according to the provisions of 135D.

A statement of illustrative matter appearing on the title page, in the preliminaries, or in the colophon that does not include the name of the artist is given only if it adds an important characterization of the material that cannot be shown in the collation; e. g. the number of illustrations in a work containing many unnumbered illustrations or the kind of illustrations (such as woodcuts or engravings). It is given as the last element of the edition area (or the next to the last element if a statement of the number of volumes is required (see 135G)). If there is no edition statement, the statement of illustrative matter is given as the last element if the title and statement of authorship area (or the next to the last element if a statement of the number of volumes is required (see 135G)).

G. Statement of the number of volumes. A statement of the number of volumes in a work is specified only if such a statement appearing on the work is at a variance with the

information shown in the collation of the work (see 141C4).
The discrepancy is explained in a note. The statement, transcribed as it appears on the title page, forms the last element
of the edition area.   If there is no edition statement it is
given as the last element of the title and statement of authorship area.

> The childermass / by Wyndham Lewis. Part 1. -- St.
> Clair Shores, Mich. : Scholarly Press, 1971.
> 322 p. ; 21 cm.
> No more published.
> Reprint of the 1928 ed. published by Covici, Friede,
> New York

For Chinese, Japanese, or Korean works issued in unnumbered fascicles (see 141C), with the text in the traditional
bibliographical divisions (i. e. chüan, kan, kwŏn) the numbering of these divisions is given immediately following the title
except when it can be more satisfactorily shown in a contents
note. The numbering is also given if necessary to distinguish
between different editions or versions of the text.

136. Imprint area

Preliminary note.   The place of publication, name of
the publisher, date of publication, and, in certain cases, the
place of printing and the name of the printer (see 140), which
constitute the imprint of a work, serve both to identify and
to characterize the work and sometimes to indicate where it
is available.   Different editions are most commonly distinguished by the differences in their imprints.

A. Order and source of elements. The imprint is recorded in the catalog entry in the conventional order of place, publisher, date, followed by the place of printing and the name of the printer when required (see 140). Imprint data taken from a source other than the title page, the preliminaries, or the colophon are enclosed in brackets. If the original imprint data in the work are covered by a label bearing different imprint data, the data so covered are recorded if legible; the imprint data on the label are recorded in a note (see 143D3e). If the original data cannot be read, the data on the label are recorded in the imprint area and the source is stated in a note (see 143D3e). If the imprint data must be supplied from a source outside the work itself, a form in the language of the title page is employed if available. Search in other sources for imprint information is made only after considering the importance of the work being cataloged and the nature of the data to be sought, the most important of the three elements of the imprint being the date.[10] (For use of the printer's imprint see 140.)

B. Punctuation

1. The place of publication is separated

---

10. It is the policy of the Library of Congress to make no search for the imprint when cataloging offprints, detached copies, or dissertations, except that when neither the publication date nor the date of the degree for which the dissertation was submitted is available it may be advisable to seek the date of publication.

a. from the name of the publisher by a space-colon
-space (:)

b. from another place of publication by a space-semicolon-space (;)

2. The name of the publisher is separated

a. from the date by a comma-space (,)

b. from the name of another place of publication by a
space-semicolon-space (;)

c. from the name of another publisher or the name of a
distributor by a space-colon-space (:)

3. The date is followed by a period unless the place and
name of the printer are required. In that case the period is
omitted.

4. The place of printing and the name of the printer are
enclosed in parentheses. Within the parentheses the same
punctuation is used for the place of printing and the name of
the printer as is used for the place of publication and the
name of the publisher (see 1 and 2 above).

Examples of punctuation of the imprint area:

Place of publication : name of publisher, date.
Place of publication ; place of publication : name of
publisher, date.
Place of publication : name of publisher : name of
publisher or distributor, date.
Place of publication : name of publisher ; place of
publication : name of publisher, date.
Place of publication : name of publisher, date (place
of printing : name of printer)

C. Works with more than one place and publisher

1. A work that gives indication of being published in several places by one publisher or by several publishers, is generally described in the catalog entry by an imprint consisting of the first named place of publication and the corresponding publisher. If, however, a place or publisher that is not the first named is distinguishable by type or position, or otherwise, as the actual or principal place or publisher, it is given in the catalog entry; in this case the first-named place or publisher is omitted. The decision is not normally to be influenced by the place of printing.

2. In the case of Japanese works, usually pre-Meiji, containing the names of several publishers, the last-named publisher, or the one with the word or words " 藏版 ," " 板 ," " 梓 ," etc., or the seal, and the appropriate place, are preferred unless there is reason to use another.

3. If a city in the country of the cataloging agency, with or without a corresponding publisher, is named in a secondary position in a work containing a foreign imprint, that information is included in addition to the foreign imprint.

> London ; New York : Longmans, Green,
> Paris : Gauthier-Villars ; Chicago : University of
>   Chicago Press,
> London : Faber ; Toronto : Cooper & Beatty,
> London : Oxford University Press ; Berkeley : University of California Press,
>   (On publication: London, Oxford
>   University Press, in association with the
>   University of California Press, Berkeley)

D. Photographically reproduced reprint and facsimile editions with only the original title page. If a photographically reproduced reprint or a facsimile edition contains only the original title page or only the original title page to which the reprint publisher's imprint has been added, the imprint of the publisher of the reprint or the facsimile, supplied in brackets if not found on the title page, in the preliminaries, or in the colophon, is given in the imprint area. The original imprint is given in a note.

Spartanburg, S. C. : Reprint Corp. , 1967.

Reprint of the 1829 ed. published by Carey, Lee & Carey, Philadelphia.

E. Fictitious imprints. If a publication bears a fictitious imprint, the actual imprint, if known, is supplied in the imprint area. If the actual imprint is not known, the abbreviations "s. l." (see 137A) and "s. n." (see 138A) are recorded in brackets in the imprint area. The fictitious imprint is recorded in a note, in the prescribed order if possible.

[Bruxelles : Moens, 1883]

Fictitious imprint on t. p. : Paris : Impr. Vincent, 1798.

[Londres : s. n.], 1771.

Fictitious imprint on t. p. : Imprimé a cent lieues de la Bastille.

[s. l. : s. n.], 1786.

Fictitious imprint on t. p. : Villefranche : Chez la Veuve Liberté.

F. Inflections in imprint. Place names or names of publishers appearing in the imprint in an inflected form or with an accompanying preposition which affects the case ending of the name are so recorded in the catalog entry. (See also 138).

>Berolini :
>V Praze :
>Im Deutschen Verlag,

137. Place of publication

Preliminary note. The place of publication is the place in which the offices of the publisher are located.

A. Place unknown. If the place of publication is unknown, the probable place of publication is given, enclosed in brackets. The probable place may be the editorial office, the seat of the institution, or the headquarters of the society publishing the work. If the probable place of publication cannot be determined, the place is represented by the abbreviation "s. l. " (sine loco) enclosed in brackets.

B. Additions to place names. The place of publication is followed by its country, state, or similar designation if it is necessary to identify the place or to distinguish it from another place of the same name. Abbreviations are used for most such designations (see Appendix III). Similarly, if the place of publication is a section or a suburb of a city, the name of the city may have to be added.

C. Abbreviated place names. If the name of the city is abbreviated in the imprint on the title page, the abbreviated

form is recorded unless the full form is found in the preliminaries or in the colophon; in that case the full form is
substituted. If the full form is not found in these sources,
the abbreviated form is completed or is followed by the full
form in brackets, e.g.

Rio [de Janeiro] :
Mpls [i.e. Minneapolis] :

D. Changed place names. If the place of publication that
is supplied has changed its name, the name that the city had
at the time the work was published is used. If the name of
the place of publication is changed, or if the place is incorporated into a larger unit during the publication of a work in
several volumes, the form of the name appearing on the first
volume, followed (in parentheses) by the later name or names
appearing on succeeding volumes, is used.

Christiania (Oslo) :

138. Publisher

A. General rule. The publisher statement appearing
on a work is abridged as much as possible without loss of
intelligibility or identification of the publisher at the international level. Unnecessary parts of the statement are omitted,
abbreviations are employed (see Appendix III), and names
known to be forenames are represented by initials[11] or,

---

11. Forenames of persons in whose honor a firm is named
are spelled in full; for example, Stephen Daye Press, not
S. Daye Press.

in the case of well-known publishers, omitted. If the personal name of the publisher is sufficient for intelligibility, and for identification of the publisher, it is given in the nominative case if it appears in that form or can be converted to it by omitting the case ending; the name is not converted if adding letters would be necessary. If the name of the publisher is unknown, the abbreviation "s. n." (sine nomine) is substituted in brackets.

> London : [s. n.],
> [s. l. : s. n.],

B. Essential parts of the publisher statement. Data that are considered necessary for the intelligibility of the publisher statement include the following:

1) Words or phrases indicating that the name in the imprint is not that of the publisher. (For use of the printer's name see 140.)

> Distributed by New York Graphic Society,
> In Kommission bei O. Harrassowitz,

2) The names of both bodies when responsibility is divided, as when one has responsibility for editorial supervision and the other for publishing or when one is the publisher and the other the distributor. Words indicating the relationship are transcribed as found in the publisher statement. If several distributors are named only the first is given unless he is not in the country of the cataloging agency and one of the others

is; in that case only the latter is given.

> London : The Society : sold by Longman,
> [Buffalo] : Mathematical Association of America ;
> [New York] : distributed by Prentice-Hall,
> Washington : Library of Congress : for sale by the
> Supt. of Docs., U. S. Govt. Print. Off.,
> London : Published for the Historical Association by
> Routledge & Paul,

3) In the case of works from the sixteenth through the eighteenth and early nineteenth centuries, before the functions of printer, publisher, and bookseller had assumed their modern differentiation, the statement of responsibility for the production of the work, transcribed as it is found in the work and in the position allocated to the publisher.

> [London] : Printed by J. Roberts,
> London : Printed by J. Wolfe for W. Wright,
> London : B. Lintott,
> (On publication: Printed for Ber. Lintott)
> London : Printed by W. Boyer and J. Nichols, and
> sold by W. Owen,

4) The name of the publishing body in the language or script of the title proper when the publishing body's name appears in several languages or scripts. If none of the languages or scripts in the imprint corresponds to the language or script of the title proper, the publishing body's name in the language or script appearing first is recorded.

C. Unnecessary parts of the publisher statement

1. The following parts are generally considered unnecessary:

a) the phrases "published by," "published for," and the word "publisher," and their equivalents in other languages when the name of a single firm is given in the work,

b) words showing that the publisher is also the printer, bookseller, or distributor,

c) the initial article, except when necessary for clarity,

d) the phrases "and company," " and sons," etc., and their foreign equivalents,

e) terms meaning "incorporated" or "limited" and their abbreviations,

f) either the name of the press or the name of the publisher if both are used, the second named generally being omitted,

g) the name of the publishing firm if it is used with the name of a branch or division which is adequately identified by its own name; e. g. McGraw-Hill and its branch, Whittlesey House,

h) the name of the director or founder of a publishing concern, and

j) either the initialism (or the abbreviation) of a corporate name or the name it represents if they are used together, the full form being omitted if it appears in any other place in the catalog entry.

2. If a Japanese work gives both the name of the publishing firm and the name of the publisher, the firm name is

usually omitted for pre-Meiji works, the name of the publisher for later works.

D. Publisher as author. When the publisher (person or corporate body) is the author of the work, and the name appears in the title and statement of authorship area (see 134B3 and 134D), the name may be given in abbreviated form in the imprint. In the case of a corporate body the abbreviation may be the initialism of the body or, if there is no widely used initialism and the usage of the language permits, the abbreviation may consist of the generic word in the name preceded by the definite article, e. g. The Society, Die Gesellschaft. Similarly, if the publisher is a subordinate unit of a corporate body only the generic word in the name of the unit is given whenever possible. Brackets are not required provided some form of the name appears on the title page, in the preliminaries, or in the colophon.

    Shadow dance / by Henry Clive Mackeson. --
London : Mackeson, 1971.
    Health today / issued by the World Health Organization. -- Geneva : WHO, 1970.
    BCG assessment in Iraq, Jordan, and Lebanon / World Health Organization, Tuberculosis Research Office. -- Copenhagen : The Office, 1957.

139. Date

A. General rule. The date is the year of publication of the first impression of the edition. In the case of a reprint by another publisher, the date is the year of publication of the first impression of the reprint edition. If it is supplied from a source other than the title page, preliminaries, or colophon it is enclosed in brackets. If there is no evidence to the contrary, either in the publication or elsewhere, the date on the title page is taken to be the date of the edition. The date may be followed by the date of a later impression, qualified by the word "printing" (without brackets), if there is a difference and if it is important to identify a later impression as such, e. g. because it contains textual variations.

1969, 1971 printing.

The date on the title page is always recorded. If the date is known to be incorrect, the correct date is added (in brackets if it does not appear in the preliminaries or in the colophon).

1975 i. e. 1957.

If the date on the title page is the date of a later impression, it is given following the publication date, qualified to show its position on the publication.

1970, t. p. 1973.

If the cover date varies from the date on the title page both dates are recorded unless the cover date is known to be the true date of publication or the date of a later impression. In these cases the cover date is recorded as a correction or as the date of a later impression.

1873, cover 1875.

If the publication date of the first impression of the

edition cannot be ascertained, the copyright date, preceded by a "c," or the date of the impression in hand, in that order of preference, or both, are given.

    c1969.
    1969 printing.
    c1969, 1971 printing.

B. Multiple volume works. If the work is in more than one volume and the imprint dates of the individual volumes vary, the inclusive dates are given. This rule is applied also if the volumes are irregularly dated. Inclusive dates in the same century are given in the form 1923-1930.

C. Loose-leaf volumes and works published in parts. If the work is a loose-leaf volume designed to receive additions, or is a work issued in parts, and is cataloged while the work is in progress of being published, the date is left open; e.g. 1944-   . When the entry is closed the inclusive dates are shown. A later title page replacing the original one may require that the date be changed, the form becoming 1946 [i.e. 1944]-1947, or 1947 [i.e. 1944-1947].

D. Dates not of the Christian era. Dates not of the Christian era are recorded as given in the publication, or in a reference source (except that Western-style Arabic numerals are substituted for oriental numerals in the cataloging of oriental materials--cf. Appendix IVF) followed by the equivalent date of the Christian era in brackets. The date of the non-Christian era is bracketed according to the provisions of

139A. If the precise year in the Christian era cannot be determined because the years in the two systems begin on different days and the month and day of publication are not known, the form "1881 or 1882" is used. Dates which are uncertain are given in the Christian era only. If one of the inclusive dates of a multiple volume work is uncertain both dates are given in the Christian era only. Similarly if the earliest or the latest volume of a multiple volume work is published with a date in the Christian era only, both of the inclusive dates are given only in the Christian era.

> Roma : [s.n.], anno XVIII [1939]
> 5730 [1969 or 1970]
> [1330 i.e. 1951 or 1952]
>   (Date from reference source)

E. Chronograms. If the date occurs as a chronogram in the title or in the imprint it is transcribed as it appears. If the chronogram is lengthy or involved it is omitted. In either case the date is supplied in brackets in Arabic numerals in the imprint. For example, if the imprint date is revealed in a chronogram reading "to aLL MarshaLLs aLL oVer the VVorLD I beqVeath thIs VVork gratIs," the date 1883 is supplied. This date was obtained by considering the large capitals to be Roman numerals and by adding them together.

F. Date uncertain. If the publication date of the first impression of the edition, the copyright date, or the date of the impression in hand cannot be ascertained, an approximate date is supplied as follows:

[1892 or 1893] one of two years certain
[1892?] probable date
[ca. 1892] approximate date
[between 1906 and 1912]
[189-] decade certain
[189-?] decade uncertain
[18--] century certain
[18--?] century uncertain

G. Copyright date. If the date in the copyright statement is not the same as the date of publication of the first impression of the edition, both dates are given. If there is more than one copyright date in a work, the latest date is chosen, except that copyright dates applying to only a part of a work and renewal dates are ignored.

1946, c1945.
[1946] c1945.
1947-1948, c1946-1948.
[196-] c1940.

H. Other qualified dates. If the date of publication of the first impression of the edition, the copyright date, the date of the impression in hand, or the approximate date is not available, but the prefatory or other matter, such as an introduction, letter of transmittal, or epilogue, is dated, this date may be used in the imprint. It must be preceded by a term which shows that it is not necessarily the date of publication (e. g. [pref. 1889]) or be followed by a question mark. Any term, English or foreign, may be used in the imprint to qualify the date if it is taken from the work being cataloged and consists of a single word. If a phrase is required to explain the questioned date, it is given in a note. If a qualified date is not a year of the Christian era the provisions of 139D are followed.

[pref. 5730 i. e. 1969 or 1970]

140. Printer's imprint. If the place of publication and the name of the publisher are unknown, the place of printing and the name of the printer are given if they appear in the work. Phrases indicating the official status of a government printer or the official authorization of a commercial printer are in- cluded.

[s. l. : s. n. , 1937] ([Boston] : Merrymount Press)

"Privately printed. "

[s. l. : s. n.], 1971 (London : Wiggs)
[s. l. : s. n.], 1935 (Ann Arbor : Edwards Bros.)
[s. l. : s. n.], 1923 (Denver : Estes Bros. , State printers)

If more than one place of printing and/or more than one print- er appear in the work, they are recorded according to the provisions of 136C. It should be noted that some presses act also as publishers and are then recorded as such, e. g. Claren- don Press, Imprimerie nationale.

141. Collation area

Preliminary note. The collation is the cataloger's de- scription of the physical work and consists of a statement of the extent of the work in pages, volumes, or volumes and

47

pages, the important illustrative matter, the size, and accompanying materials, if any. The general aims of a collation statement are i) to present a picture of the physical characteristics of the work to the reader, so as to assist him both in identifying the work and telling him something of its nature, ii) to assist in showing how various editions of a work differ from each other, and iii) to ensure that all those parts of the work are described which would be retained in the binding or rebinding of the work. The terms used are those for which accepted definitions are available rather than those of the author or publisher, if there is any conflict between the two.

A. Punctuation

1. The volume and/or pagination statement is separated

a. from the illustration statement by a space-colon-space (:)

b. from the size statement by a space-semicolon-space (;)

2. The illustration statement is separated from the size statement by a space-semicolon-space (;)

3. The size statement is separated

a. from the series statement by a period-space-dash--space (. --)

b. from the statement of accompanying materials by a space-ampersand-space (&)

4. The statement of accompanying materials is separated

from the series statement by a period-space-dash-space
(. --)

Examples of punctuation of the collation area:

Number of volumes and/or pages : illustration statement ; size & accompanying material. --
Number of volumes and/or pages ; size. --

B. Extent of text in one volume

1. General rules

a. In describing the extent of a work that is complete in
one volume, the terminology suggested by the work is followed as far as possible. That is, a work with leaves printed
on both sides is described in terms of pages, one with the
leaves printed on only one side, in terms of leaves. A work
which has numbered pages and unnumbered leaves is described only in terms of pages, one that has numbered leaves
and unnumbered pages is described only in terms of leaves.
A work without numbering is described in terms of either
pages or leaves, but not of both. Books printed before the
eighteenth century, or photoreproductions of them, with leaves
printed on both sides but numbered as leaves are described
in terms of leaves. A work printed with more than one
column to a page, the columns instead of the pages being
numbered, is described in terms of columns. A folder,
a broadside, a sheet and a roll are so called in the collation.

b. In recording the number of pages, leaves, or columns,
the indication in the work (whether Roman or Arabic numbers,

or letters) is followed.   In describing a work with pages lettered rather than numbered, the inclusive letters are specified; for example, p. a-x, or p. A-K, or leaves a-d.   Pages or leaves numbered in words, or in characters other than Arabic or Roman, are designated in the collation in Arabic figures.

c.   The last numbered page or leaf of each numbered section is recorded, the numbers being separated by commas. A section is either a separately numbered group of pages, or leaves, or an unnumbered group which, because of its length (one fifth or more of the entire work), or its importance, should be mentioned.   The figure representing the unnumbered group is enclosed in brackets.   Separately numbered and unnumbered sections consisting of advertising matter are disregarded (see 141B11).   If it is necessary to refer in a supplementary note to unnumbered pages or leaves that would not otherwise be covered by the collation, the collation is elaborated to include the unnumbered group of pages or leaves.

```
     86, [1] p. :
     Bibliography: p. [87]
     365, [3] p. :
     Bibliography: p. 363-[367]
     [8], 155 p. :
     Bibliography: 6th prelim. page
```

d.   The number of leaves of plates is given at the end of the sequences of pagination, whether the plates are found together in the publication or are distributed throughout the work, or even if there is only one plate, such as a frontispiece. More than one illustration on a leaf, even if numbered by the printer, does not affect the numeration of the plates as such.

> xvi, 246 p., 24 leaves of plates :
> x, 32, 73 p., [12] leaves of plates :
> vii, [35] p., 12 leaves of plates :
> x, 321 p., [1] leaf of plates :

e. If the last numbered page or leaf does not represent the total number, or approximately the total number, of pages or leaves in the work or in the section, a correction may be necessary. For example, (a) if only the alternate pages are numbered the collation may read 48 [i.e. 96] p., (b) if the final page is typographically incorrect, the collation may read 329 [i.e. 392] p. If the numbering changes from Roman to Arabic numerals within the sequence this fact is ignored. For example, a work with pages numbered i-viii, 9-176 is described simply as 176 p. Inclusive paging is given for works that seem to be incomplete or which are merely parts of a larger work.

> p. 89-149 :
> p. 11-278 :
> leaves 56-75 :

2. Unpaged works. If a work in one volume printed without pagination or foliation contains 100 pages or leaves

or less, they are counted[12] and the number is enclosed in brackets.

>[87] p. :
>[46] leaves :

If the work contains more than 100 pages or leaves, they may be counted or approximated to the nearest multiple of 50.

>ca. 500 p. :
>ca. 250 leaves :

3. Complicated or irregular paging. Either of two ways of describing works with complicated or irregular paging may be chosen depending upon the extent of the complications:

a. If a publication contains no more than three numbered main sections accompanied by lesser variously numbered or unnumbered sections, the number of pages or leaves in each of the main sections is recorded and the total number of the remaining variously numbered and unnumbered sections is added in brackets.

>xiv, 226, [44] p. :

b. If a publication contains more than three numbered main sections, the numbers on the last numbered page or leaf of each section are added and the total is given followed by the words "in various pagings" or "in various foliations. "

---

12. The count begins with the first printed page and ends with the last printed page, exclusive of advertising matter; intermediate blank pages and leaves are counted.

968 p. in various pagings :
not 48, 53, 99, 268, 410, 90 p. :

c. A loose-leaf publication intended to receive additional or substituted pages or leaves and consisting of one volume at the time of cataloging, is described as 1 v. (even though the pagination or foliation is not complicated or irregular) unless there is evidence that it is to appear in several volumes. In that case the statement of the number of volumes is left open. The following note is given:

Loose-leaf for updating.

4. Folded leaves. Folded leaves of text or plates are so described unless the work is bibliographically unimportant.

17 fold. leaves :
[37] leaves (3 fold.) :
xvii, 341 p., 32 fold. leaves of plates :

5. Double leaves. If numbered pages are printed on a double leaf, Chinese and Japanese style, they are described as pages or leaves according to their numbering as pages or leaves; if unnumbered, each double leaf is counted as two pages.

36 p. (on double leaves) :
18 double leaves :
[36] p. (on double leaves) :

6. Duplicate paging. If the paging is duplicated, which is not unusual in books with text in two languages, both pagings are recorded and an explanation is added.

xii, 35, 35 p. :
Opposite pages numbered in duplicate.

7. Two numberings. If a work has a pagination of its own and also bears the pagination of a larger work of which it is a part, the separate paging is recorded in the collation and the continuous paging in a supplementary note.

Pages also numbered 35-89 continuing the paging of the preceding number.

8. Two-way paging. In the case of works with groups of pages numbered in opposite directions, as in works with texts in two languages, the pagings of the various sections are recorded in straight sequence starting from the title page selected for cataloging.

ix, 115, 127, x p. :

9. Columns. If an unpaged work is printed in numbered columns, two or more to a page, the number of columns is given in the collation.

xx p., 1660 columns :

10. Music in collation. If, in a work which is not entirely music, an unpaged or separately paged or foliated section consists of music, these pages or leaves are designated as music in collation, following the number of pages of text.

74 p., 15 p. of music :

If the music occurs in scattered groups of pages or leaves not independently numbered, it is generally described in a supplementary note rather than in the collation.

11. Advertisements in collation. If a section of advertising matter follows the text of a work and is continuously
paged or foliated with the text, the inclusive pagination or
foliation of the advertising matter is designated in the collation following the number of pages or leaves of text, enclosed
in parentheses.

124 p. (p. 119-124 advertisements) :

12. Incomplete copies. If the last part of a work is
wanting, and the paging of a complete copy cannot be ascertained, paging is given in the form 179+ p., with note of the
imperfection.

xxiv, 179+ p. :
Imperfect copy: all after p. 179 wanting.

C. Extent of text in more than one volume

1. The number of bibliographical volumes or parts of a
work in more than one volume is shown in the collation. If
this number differs from the number of physical volumes,
both are stated, the bibliographical volumes first.

8 v. in 5 :

2. If the work is paged continuously, the pagination is
indicated, in parentheses, following the number of volumes,
according to the rule for indicating the pagination of a work
that is complete in one volume. Separately paged preliminary matter in volumes after the first is ignored unless it is

important; if it is important, the work is not considered as being paged continuously.

    2 v. (xxxi, 999 p.) :
    3 v. (xx, 1120 p., 150 leaves of plates) :

3. Works in more than one volume that are printed on double leaves are so described.

    2 v. (on double leaves) :

4. If a work is planned for more than one volume, but only one has been published and it appears that no more will be published, the paging, rather than the number of volumes, is given in the collation. (The volume number is given in the body of the entry (see 135G) and a note, "No more published," is made.)

5. In addition to volumes, the following terms are used in the collation to describe works in more than one volume or part:

Parts--for bibliographical units of a work intended to be bound several to the volume, especially if so designated by the publisher.

Pamphlets--for the collections of pamphlets bound together or assembled for cataloging as a collection.

Pieces--for items of varying character (pamphlets, broadsides, clippings, maps, etc.) published or assembled for cataloging as a collection.

Cases--1) for boxes specially dimensioned to the bound or

unbound material they contain; 2) for Oriental-style portfolios, normally cloth-covered, containing fascicles.

Portfolios--for containers holding loose papers, illustrative material, etc.

6. In the case of works in unusual formats, e.g. paper discs in a can, a term which appropriately describes the work is used.

D. Illustrative matter

1. General rule

a. Brief mention of the illustrative matter in a work comprises the second part of the collation statement. The abbreviation "ill.," for illustrations, is used to describe all types of illustrative matter unless particular types in the work are considered important enough to be specifically designated.[13] When particular types are important, they are designated by the following terms in alphabetical order: coats of arms, diagrams, facsimiles, forms, genealogical tables, graphs, maps, music, plans, portraits (or group portraits, but not both), samples. (See Appendix III, Abbreviations) When both illustrations and one or more particular types of

13. It is the policy of the Library of Congress to use only the term "ill." so long as the types of illustrations in a particular work follow the conventional pattern of illustration for works of the particular category, e.g. histories, treatises on physics. However, if it can be readily determined that a work contains only one type of illustrative matter, the specific term is used.

illustrative matter are included, the abbreviation "ill." is given first. If the illustrative matter is limited to an illustrated title page or to minor illustration, it is generally disregarded.

b. Tables are considered to be textual matter and are not mentioned in the collation area unless it is necessary to specify material in pockets, portfolios, etc. (see 5 and F below). If a work consists entirely or chiefly of tables, they are mentioned in a note, unless their presence is clearly implied by the wording of the title and statement of authorship area.

> Tables.
> Chiefly tables.

2. Colored illustrative matter. Important illustrative matter that is printed with ink in two or more colors (counting black as a color), or some of which is so printed, is described as colored.[14]

> col. ill., maps (some col.), col. ports. ;

3. Illustrative matter on folded leaves. The fact that illustrative matter is printed on folded leaves is generally disregarded unless the folding is especially significant, e.g. a panoramic view.

---

14. The Library of Congress notes the presence of colored illustrative matter only when color is of particular importance, e.g. in art books, natural history guides, children's books.

fold. col. facsim. ;

4. Number of illustrations recorded. The number of illustrations, portraits, maps, etc., may be specified in the collation if the illustrations, etc. are numbered or if the number can readily be ascertained (i.e. when the illustrations are listed). Arabic numerals are used. Brackets are not used to indicate that the numerals do not appear on the illustrations. See 135F for the treatment of statements of the number of illustrations appearing on the title page or in the preliminaries. See 141Bld for provisions for recording the number of plates.

5. Illustrative matter in pockets

a. Illustrative matter, issued in a pocket inside the cover of a work, is mentioned in the collation and its location designated. The number of separate pieces is generally specified.

> 3 graphs (in pocket) ;
> ill., maps (4 fold. col. in pocket) ;
> 100 col. maps (2 fold in pocket) ;

b. If, however, more than one type of illustration specified in the collation is represented wholly or in part by items in the pocket, a general note is used instead.

> Illustrative matter in pocket.
> Part of illustrative matter in pocket.

6. Illustrative matter on lining papers. The location of a map or other illustrative matter printed on the lining paper or papers is specified in the collation if it is the only map

or other illustrative matter of its type in the work.

    187 p. : geneal. table (on lining paper), ports. ;

    7. Illustrations with little or no text. If the work consists entirely or chiefly of illustrations, this fact is noted in the illustration statement.

    500 p. : all ill. ;
    120 p. : chiefly ill., maps, ports. ;
    1 portfolio ([2] leaves, 72 leaves of plates : 72 ill.) ;
    2 portfolios : chiefly ill. ;

    E. Size

Preliminary note. The size of the work is included in the catalog entry as an aid in finding the work on the shelves and as an aid to the user of the catalog in selecting a desirable edition. It also serves the reader who wishes to borrow the work through interlibrary loan or who wishes to order a photocopy of the work or a part of it.

    1. The height of the work is given in centimeters, exact to within one centimeter, fractions of a centimeter being counted as a full centimeter. For example, a work which measures 17.2 centimeters is described as 18 cm. Miniature books, those ten centimeters or less in height, are described in millimeters, exact to the nearest millimeter. In describing bound volumes, the height of the binding is measured. In describing a pamphlet inserted in a binder, the height of the pamphlet is given.

    2. The width of the work is also specified if it is less

than half the height or if it is greater than the height. The height is given first, in the following form: 20 x 8 cm. or 20 x 32 cm.

3. Both height and width are specified in the collation of broadsides and other single sheets. If the sheet is designed for issue in folded format, as indicated by data on outside when folded, or by part of the material being imposed as pages, the dimensions of the sheet as folded are also given, in the following form: 48 x 30 cm. fold. to 24 x 15 cm. If the sheet is intended to be used only in the folded form, it is described as a folder, followed by the number of imposed pages, rather than as a sheet; only the folded size is given.

folder (8 p.) ; 18 cm. --

4. If there is a difference of less than two centimeters in the size of the volumes of a set, the larger size is given in the collation. If the difference is of two or more centi- meters, the inclusive sizes are given, e.g. 24-27 cm.

5. In cataloging a volume consisting of pamphlets or other works of different size bound together, the size of the bound volume is given.

6. In the case of works in unusual formats, e. g. boxes or cans, two or three dimensions are given as necessary to indicate the space occupied by the work. The dimension which represents the height of the work as it stands on the shelf is given first.

F. Accompanying materials

Preliminary note. The fourth element of the collation area is a description of material accompanying the work being cataloged and intended to be used in conjunction with it. Such materials include answer books, teacher's manuals, etc. not important enough to require a more detailed description; atlases or portfolios of plates not numbered consecutively with other volumes of the set; and audiovisual materials, e. g. those typically placed in pockets on the cover of the work.

1. Accompanying material is described in terms of a word or phrase indicating the nature of the material.

271 p. : ill. ; 21 cm. & answer book. --

2. If further description is desired, as in the case of atlases and portfolios of plates, a statement of the extent of the publication and of the illustrative material it contains is given within parentheses after the characterizing term. Within the parentheses the same punctuation pattern is used as is prescribed for other parts of the collation area. If the size of the atlas or portfolio differs from the size of the work it accompanies, the size is included in the description.

3 v. ; 30 cm. & atlas (301 leaves of plates : ill.). --
271 p. : ill. ; 21 cm. & atlas (37 p., 19 leaves of plates : 19 col. maps ; 37 cm.). --
3 leaves, 100 p. : ill. ; 25 cm. & portfolio (24 leaves of plates : ill. ; 30 cm.). --
6 v. : ill., maps ; 22 cm. & atlases (3 v. : ill., maps). --
9 v. in 11 : ill., maps ; 26 cm. & atlas (2 v. : maps). --

In the case of audiovisual materials the physical description of the materials is given according to the provision of chapters 12 and 14.

> 124 p. ; 31 cm. & phonodisc (2 s. : 12 in. ; 33 1/3 rpm. microgroove) in pocket. --
> xi, 396 p. ; 19 cm. & phonodiscs (6 s. : 12 in. ; 78 rpm.). --
> iv, 196 p. ; 21 cm. & phonodiscs (2 albums (10 s.)) : 12 in. ; 78 rpm.). --
> xi, 246 p. ; 20 cm. & slides (20 slides : col. ; 2x2 in.) in pockets. --

3. If, however, the title of the accompanying material differs from that of the main work, or if there is a special compiler, or if some other features require further description, the form of entry adopted for supplements is preferred (see 155).

142. Series area

A. General rules

1. A series statement, i.e. a statement of the collective title under which a work is issued as one of its parts, is transcribed enclosed in parentheses.[15] If the statement or any part of it does not appear anywhere in the work being cataloged, and is supplied from another source (as when it has been inadvertently omitted from the work), the part is

---

15. It is sometimes difficult to determine whether a phrase on the title page or elsewhere in the publication is a publisher's name, a series statement, a subtitle, or simply a publisher's characterization of some or all of his books (e. g. A Borzoi book). In case of doubt it is preferable to give such a phrase as a quoted note; or, if it merely provides

supplied, enclosed in brackets. If the entire series statement is supplied, it is enclosed in brackets within parentheses. In the case of reprints by another publisher which mention a series in which the edition being reprinted was originally published, that series is recorded in a note. Series statements appearing only on dust jackets are generally ignored.

The series statement on the work may include, in addition to the title of the series (in one or more languages), the name of a personal or corporate author or authors or of an editor or editors, and the number of the volume if the series consists of consecutively numbered volumes or parts. The series area generally includes all of this information except the names of editors. If the series has a subtitle, the latter is omitted unless it is necessary for identification; when given it is separated from the title by a comma. If the series title appears in more than one language or script, one of which agrees with the language or script of the title proper, only this title is given in the series area.[16] If

a variant identification of the publisher, (e. g. A Halsted Press book; publisher: Halsted Press) it may be ignored. If a number or a combination of numbers and letters of the alphabet which cannot be associated with a series title (e. g. No. 22; HUD6-A; 18050 DIE 12/71) appears on a publication, the number is given as a quoted note unless the publisher is a commercial publisher. In that case the number is omitted from the description.

16. National cataloging agencies record series titles in all languages or scripts in the case of publications of the home country.

the series title appears in more than one language or script none of which agrees with the language or script of the title proper only the first title is used.   The form follows the statement on the work as far as E2-3 below permit except that the number of the volume in the series is placed at the end unless this would involve a transposition affecting grammatical structure.   The number is preceded by the term used on the work to describe it unless the term is long and there is no abbreviation for it.   For terms that are abbreviated see Appendix III.

When a series has been assigned an International Standard Serial Number (ISSN), the ISSN is given as found in the publication after the title of the series and its numbering or after the title of the subseries and its numbering, preceded by a space and the letters ISSN.[17]

2. The title of the series, or of any subseries, is separated from its numbering by a space-semicolon-space (;). The statement of a main series, including any numbering, is separated from that of a subseries by a space-colon-space (:).

Examples of punctuation of the series area:

(Series ; number)
(Series : Subseries ; number)

17. In Library of Congress cataloging the ISSN's will appear whenever possible with the proper segmentation indicated by hyphens.

(Series ; number : Subseries ; number)

(Typophile chap books ; 7)
(Britain advances ; [10])
(Ergänzungsheft zum Deutschen statistischen Zentralblatt ; 7)
(Biblioteca de autores cristianos ; 7 : Serie maior ; 13)
(World history series : section 3, Europe ; v. 7)

B.   Works in several volumes.   If a work in a numbered series is in several volumes, the series volume numbers are given in an inclusive form (e. g. v. 11-15) or in a form indicating a broken sequence (e. g. v. 131, 145, 152).   If the work is in many volumes, the series volume numbers may be specified in the contents note and their omission from the series explained (see 148B11).

C.   Series title in two forms. If the series title appears on the work in more than one form, the form that is used for the entry of the series in the catalog is selected for the series area.   The variant form is noted if it appears to be of value for identification purposes.   (See 142A1 if language or script   rather than form is involved.)

D.   Series title combined with the monograph title.   A series title occurring in combination with the monograph title is separated, if possible, from the latter and given in the regular series position.

From morality to religion, being the Gifford lecture delivered at the University of St. Andrews, 1938.
Title: From morality to religion.
Series: (Gifford lecture ; 1938)

E.   Author in series statement

1. If the title   of a series is the title of a multi-volume monograph and the author of the series is the same as the author of the individual part being cataloged, the appropriate possessive pronoun is substituted for the author's name, unless the name is integrated with the series title.

> (His Wild world tales)
> (Her Brontë sources ; 2)
> (Their The corridors of time ; 8)
> (Its Publications in research and records)
> (Éditions de travail des oeuvres de Schumann)
> (The works of Charles Dickens ; 2)
> (McEvoy's essentials of geography ; 4)
> (Papers from the International Lonergan Congress, 1970 ; v. 2)

2. If the title of a series is the title of a serial and the name of the author of the series is an integral part of the series title, the name of the author is included in the series statement.

> (Public Health Service publication ; no. 1634)
> (NEA   research memo ; 1971-9)
> (Neujahrsblatt der Allgemeinen Musikgesellschaft in Zürich)
> (Historical publications of the Society of Colonial Wars in the Commonwealth of Pennsylvania)
> (Contributions de l'Institut botanique de l'Université de Montréal ; no 61)

3. If the title of a series consisting solely of a generic term is the title of a serial, the generic term is followed by the author statement.   The two elements are separated by a space-hyphen-space (-).   The author statement is transcribed as it appears on the publication except that, if the statement includes a corporate hierarchy, those parts of the hierarchy (generally intermediate) which are not necessary

for the identification of the author are omitted. The parts of

the hierarchy which are recorded are separated by commas.

> (Information series - Geological Survey of Alabama ;
> 42)
> (Special paper - Geological Society of America ;
> no. 6)
> (Parliamentary paper - The Parliament of the Common-
> wealth of Australia ; no. 254, 1973)
> (Bulletin - Commonwealth of Australia, Council for
> Scientific and Industrial Research ; no. 229)
> (Publicación - Universidad de Chile, Facultad de
> Ciencias Físicas y Matemáticas ; no. 12)
> (Publicación - Instituto de Geografía de la Universi-
> dad de Chile ; no. 2)
> (Publicación - Universidad de Chile, Departamen-
> to de Geología ; no. 28)
> (On publication: Universidad de Chile, Facultad de
> Ciencias Físicas y Matemáticas, Departamento de
> Geología)
> (Technical memorandum -   Beach Erosion Board ;
> no. 125)
> (On publication: Department of the Army, Corps of
> Engineers, Beach Erosion Board, Office of the Chief
> of Engineers)
> (Special bibliography - National Highway Traffic
> Safety Administration ; no. 2)
> (On publication: U. S. Department of Transportation,
> National Highway Traffic Safety Administration)

F.   Works in more than one series[18]

1.   If a work is a part of more than one series, all series

statements, each enclosed within its own set of parenthe-

ses, are given immediately following the collation area. The

series that is chosen for the first position is the one that

is more specialized and less extensive, if such a comparison

---

18. A series issued in two or more sequences and called
"second series, " "new series, " or by a similar designation,
has this designation included, with the customary abbreviations, as the series numbering, not as a separate subseries or

is possible.

> (East Asian and Pacific series ; 199) (Department
> of State publication ; 8583)
> (Acta antiqua et archaeologica ; 10) (Acta Universi-
> tatis Szegediensis de Attila József nominatae)
> 10 v. ; 28 cm. -- (Anthropological monographs ; no.
> 23-30) (v. 9-10: Art and anthropological monographs ;
> no. 31-32)

2. If one series is a subseries of the other, both are specified within one set of parentheses, the main series being given first.

> (Biblioteca del lavoro : Serie professionale)
> (Biblioteca de arte hispánico ; 8 : Artes aplicadas ;
> 1)

143. Notes area--General rules

A. Definition and purpose. Many works require description beyond that presented according to the preceding rules. This description may be combined with the formalized part of the entry or it may be added in the form of supplementary notes.

Additional information may be incorporated in the formalized part of the entry only to the extent that the rules for the preparation of this part of the description provide (see 130, 133-140). This limitation is necessary if the advantages of a formalized description are not to be lost. Additions may similiarly be made in the collation area when they are matters of physical description and can be stated very briefly (see 141B11, 141D5, and 141F).

Notes amplify or qualify the formalized description, either when the rules do not permit the inclusion of the needed information in any form other than a note or when the incorporation of the information in the formalized description would be misleading, cumbersome, or inappropriate.

B. Categories of notes. In general, supplementary notes fall into two categories: 1) notes that contribute in a significant way to the identification of the work or the intelligibility of the catalog entry (e.g. a note explaining the relationship to the work of a person or a corporate body for whom a secondary entry is indicated) or that are essential for the reader who does not already have in hand the exact citation to the work he is seeking, and 2) notes that characterize the work and tell its bibliographic history. Most of the notes in the first category are indispensable, regardless of the inherent value of the work being cataloged. The others, in either category, will be supplied at the discretion of the cataloger who will be guided by bibliographic considerations peculiar to the work, its relative importance, and the availability and costs of obtaining certain information.

1. Indispensable notes. Notes to provide the following types of information are generally indispensable:

a) To identify the work or edition and distinguish it from others; e.g. an edition statement that cannot be presented in the formalized part of the entry because of its length, complexity, or other consideration (see 135), or to show that the work is in microform (see 156). A note may be essential also to explain the source of the title used in the entry (e. g. title from cover), to show a variation from the title page title appearing elsewhere in the work (a variant cover title, caption title, or running title), to show variations in the title in a work of several volumes, or to provide variant or supplemental information appearing on an added title page.

b) To provide essential information regarding the authorship of the work, e. g. the names of persons to whom the work has been attributed.

c) To clarify the relationship of the heading or of an added entry to the work (often an at-head-of-title note; see 144).

d) To clarify misleading information in the formalized part of the entry; e. g. when a slip mounted on the title page supplies a correction.

e) To provide information essential to locating the work; e. g. when it is part of or bound with another work (see 157 and 145).

f) To explain that the work is incomplete or imperfect.

g) To describe accompanying material; e. g. a separate index or supplement (see 155).

h) To show the contents of a multivolume work (see 148).

j) To supply a romanized form of a title in a non-Roman script so that it can be interfiled with titles in the Roman alphabet (see 150).

2. Important but not indispensable notes. Notes to provide other types of information vary in importance and are not generally indispensable. These include notes

a) To reveal the contents or partial contents (particularly bibliographies and indexes) of a work in one volume.

b) To supplement the physical description in the collation; e.g. to show that the actual amount of text is not correctly suggested by the collation; that there is text on covers, guard sheets, plates, etc.; to show peculiarities and irregularities; to describe format, limited editions (i.e. editions consisting of 500 copies or less), large paper copies, etc.

c) To show the nature and scope of the work and its literary form if the title is misleading; literary form is not indicated for a classic nor ordinarily for fiction.

d) To show the language of the text if the language of the title differs from that of the text, or if for any other reason the language of the text is not obvious.

e) To provide bibliographical history of the work; relationship to other works, etc. (see 143D2 and 143D4).

f) To indicate that the work is a thesis or other academic

publication (see 146 and 147).

g) To provide a statement of the limited distribution or noncommercial nature of the work.

C. Style. Rules 144-148 provide fixed forms for certain notes. Informal notes are used for any other data that need to be supplied. They may take any of the following forms:

1) Quotations from the work being cataloged or from other sources;

2) Statements composed in English by the cataloger when the information cannot be given more concisely or more clearly by 1 above (the examples of notes in D below are to be taken as suggestions for the wording of cataloger's notes rather as prescribed forms for notes);

3) References to passages in the publication and to other sources if lengthy notes can thus be avoided;

4) A combination of 1-3 above.

Fixed forms are not prescribed for informal notes but the following general principles should guide the cataloger in formulating them.[19]

Notes are as brief as clarity and good grammatical usage

---

19. The Library of Congress' authority for the spelling of the words that are not quoted is the latest edition of Webster's new international dictionary of the English language. When alternative spellings are given, the first is preferred.

permit.

In notes which include imprints given in conventional order the prescribed punctuation for the imprint area is used. In other cases prescribed punctuation may be used where appropriate or conventional punctuation may be used.

Notes are factual and unbiased and do not state critical judgments of the cataloger.

The value of each note is considered in relation to the resulting length of the whole catalog entry.

Information supplied in notes is documented in accordance with the stated principles of descriptive cataloging. The form of the citation is as follows: the source of a quoted note is preceded by a dash; the source of a statement not quoted, by "Cf. " The source, not included within quotation marks, consists of the author's name, in direct form, and the title, both in sufficient fullness for identification. The author and title of a work in a non-Roman script are given only in romanized form. Commonly used and easily recognizable words are abbreviated. If page reference is given, the citation should identify the edition.

When, in notes composed by the cataloger or in notes recording bibliographical relationship (see 143D2 and 4), it is necessary to mention an author's name or a title which is in a language not written in the Roman alphabet, the name or title is given in romanized form only.

D. Order. Various considerations affect the order of notes, making an invariable order undesirable. In certain cases, various notes are combined or grouped together to produce a clear, logical entry; for example in cataloging a facsimile reproduction or a photographic reproduction to be described as such (see 156), the notes referring to the original edition are grouped and separated from notes referring specifically to the reproduction.

In general the following order will prevail:

1) Analytical note (see 157).

2) Original title note.   When the title of the edition or translation of the work being cataloged varies from the title of the original edition, the note (the first unless an analytical note is required) records the original title as indicated below:

a) The original title of a translated work. If the original title or a generally accepted variant title has been given as a uniform title preceding the title-page title or has been included in the transcription of the title and statement of authorship area (see 134C2), the note is omitted.

> Translation of I promessi sposi.
> Translation of Na dne.

b) The original or earliest known title of a work reissued in the same language with a changed title, except for the works of classical authors for which a special filing scheme has been adopted.   The statement is worded to include all earlier editions if this can be done with brevity and with-

out further search.

First ed. published in 1934 under title:
Previous editions published under title:

c) The title selected as the uniform title if the work is

published simultaneously in the same language under different

titles (see 101C1).[20]

American ed. published under title:

d) The title of a later revised or updated edition (see

100E).[20]

Second ed. published in 1960 under title:
Beginning with the 4th ed. (1932) published under

title:

---

20. Alternative rule: Libraries which do not use uniform
titles (or which use them only for particular authors) may
prefer to adopt the following rules and suggestions for forms
of notes:

c) The titles of one or more other editions in the same
language, if it cannot be ascertained which is the earlier.

New York ed. (Knopf) has title:
London ed. (Collins) has title:

d) Information that a work in a foreign language has
been issued also in English, if neither is known to be a
translation of the other.

Issued also in English.

e) The title of the edition in the language of the heading
or the native tongue of the author, if a work is issued in
several languages at the same time and without indication
of the original, unless the titles are literal translations.

Issued also under title:

e) The title selected as the uniform title if the work is published simultaneously in different languages under different titles none of which is known to be the original language and title, unless names or cognates in both make the noting of the uniform title unnecessary (see 101C2-3).[20]

Issued also under title:

3) Notes that refer to the elements of the formalized description, in the same order as they appear there.

a) Title proper.

Caption title.[21]
Cover title: The fair American.
Vol. 2 has title:

b) Other titles and title information bearing on the nature, scope, language, or literary form of the work. (See also 146 and 147.) The language, or languages, of the work are always noted if not unmistakably indicated by the wording of the title page.

Subtitle varies slightly.
An advertisement for the Bell Telephone Co.
To 1914. Later memoirs "in preparation" were not published.
Prose translation.
"An abridgement in one volume, by Richard Harwell, of the four-volume R. E. Lee."
English and German.
Hymns in Greek; commentary in Italian
    (Title page in Italian)
English, French, Russian, or Spanish with summaries in the other languages.

---

20. See page 76.

21. Not used in cataloging broadsides or other material limited to one leaf.

c) Statement of authorship. (See also 144.)

Also attributed to Jonathan Swift. Cf. Evans. Amer. bibl.
"Also attributed to Jonathan Swift."--Evans. Amer. bibl.

d) Edition area.

On cover, v. 1: 3. éd.; v. 2: 2. éd.
Translated from the author's unpublished ms.

e) Imprint area.

Imprint covered by label which reads: Humanitas-Verlag, Zürich.
Original imprint covered by label, as above.
"Privately printed."

f) Collation area and additional physical description. (See

also 145 and 155.)

Imperfect copy: t. p. wanting; title from cover.[22]
Incomplete set: v. 12 wanting.
Pages 65-98, coordinate paper [blank for "Notes, " etc.]
(Such a section is ignored unless it occupies more than one fifth of the total number of pages. (See 141B11))
Text on versos of plates.
(Such a note is used only if the paging suggests very little text and there is a relatively large amount of text on the plates)
Signatures:
(Used only to distinguish two issues or editions with the same final pagination)
Printed on vellum.
"300 copies printed in Perpetua type on Arnold's hand-made paper; no. 8."
250 copies printed. No. 64.
Reproduced from ms. copy.

4) Notes that record the bibliographical relationship to

---

22. The Library of Congress uses the form "L. C. copy imperfect: ."

other editions of the same work (other than changes of title (see 2 above)) or to other works, e. g. predecessors, successors, sequels, revisions which are substantially new works. These include:

    a) The author or editor of earlier or subsequent editions if there has been a change of author heading.

> Based on the 3d ed. of Guide to the study and use of reference books by A. B. Kroeger as revised by I. G. Mudge.

    b) The title of a work which continues the work being cataloged or the title of an earlier work which the work being cataloged continues. In the case of works of the imagination the word "sequel" is used to express the relationship.

> Sequel: Le collier de la reine.
> Sequel to Mémoires d'un médecin.

In the case of other works "continues" and "continued by, " or terms suggested by the work itself, are used.

    c) Information in regard to the original publication of works issued as reprint editions if the information is readily ascertainable. This information includes the publisher and date of the edition from which the reprint was made or, in the case of the date, unless the copyright date of the original appears in the imprint area (see 139G) and the series in which the original was published.

> Reprint of the 1910 ed. published by Houghton, Mifflin, Boston.
> Reprint of the 1945 ed. published by G. Cumberlege, London, which was issued as the Sir Israel Gollancz

memorial lecture, British Academy, 1945.

d) Information in regard to the original publication of works which first appeared as part of another publication if this can be given in a specific form leading to the earlier work (see 153A, 154A).

> From the author's Unterhaltungen deutscher Ausgewanderten.
> "Reprinted from the Physical review, vol. 70, nos. 5-6... September 1-15, 1916."

e) In the case of facsimile editions, information relating to the facsimile is given in notes arranged so that the information referring to the original work can be clearly distinguished from that referring to the facsimile edition. When a statement describing the physical form of the original is required, however, it is incorporated in the note concerning the facsimile, if there is one.

1) If a statement that a work is a facsimile edition does not appear in the title and statement of authorship area, the edition area, or the series area, that fact is recorded in a note.

> Facsim. ed.

If, on the other hand, a work which is presented as a facsimile edition does not meet the requirements of the definition of a facsimile edition and the statement that the work is a facsimile is of such a nature that it must be recorded in the title and statement of authorship area, the edition area, or the series area, a note is provided to indicate that the work is merely a photoreprint.

> Photoreprint ed.

2) Other notes may be required to provide:

A transcription of all or a portion of the original title page if necessary to record essential data which do not otherwise appear in the entry. The words "Includes original t. p. :" introduce the note. Omissions are shown by the mark of omission (...).

The location of the copy from which a facsimile edition has been made, if the copy has unique characteristics which make it worthy of note.

> Facsim. of the Huntington Library copy, which has
> ms. notes by R. Heber on flyleaves.

If, however, the work in hand is a photoreprint, the words "Photoreprint ed." are substituted for the word "Facsim."

The location of the manuscript copy from which a facsimile has been made.

> The first play in the so-called "Parnassus trilogy"
> reproduced in facsim. from a unique ms. in the
> Bodleian Library (Rawlinson D. 398).

The manuscript source of a work if such information is essential in identifying the work.

> The original ms., IV. A. 3 in the Biblioteca nazionale,
> Naples, contains the second and only remaining portion
> of the abridgment by Festus of the lost treatise, De ver-
> borum significatu, of M. Verrius Flaccus.

5) Contents (see 148).

144. "At head of title" note

Information that appears at the head of the title and is not transposed to another position in the catalog entry (as series, author statement, subtitle, edition, etc.) is noted in the form of a conventional note beginning with the phrase, "At head of title."

Information noted in this fashion includes the names of corporate bodies whose relationship to the work as sponsor or issuing body is unknown or cannot be concisely stated, statements that seem to be neither series nor subtitle, and any other information that is not provided for by the general pattern of the catalog entry. This note is generally the first note unless an analytical note (see 157), an "original title" note (see 143D2), or a note specifying the source of the title data is required.

a) Different form of author's name from that in the heading.

Author's name in Chinese at head of title.

b) Corporate body not chosen as author heading although named at head of title.

At head of title: República de Chile. Armada Nacional. (Entry: Chile. Laws, statutes, etc.)
At head of title: International Labour Organisation. (Entry: International Labor Conference, 27th, Paris, 1945)
At head of title: Istituto di zootecnia della Università di Milano.

(Entry: Piana, Giuseppe)

c) <u>Initials, seal, or other insignia indicating the neces-</u>
<u>sity for an added entry.</u>

> Seal of State of Minnesota Forest Service at head of
> title.

d) <u>Miscellaneous types of data not included in the body</u>
<u>of the entry.</u>

> At head of title: Confidential.
> At head of title: Junior high school, remedial reading.
> At head of title: They came from Ireland.
> (Entry: Judson, Clara Ingram. Michael's victory)

145. Notes of works bound together

A. If two or more distinct works, each with its own title
page and paging, are issued together in one cover, or if several works issued independently are subsequently bound
together, the entry for each work in the volume bears a
note to show the presence of the other work or works. For
the first work in the volume, the note is simply a matter of
of physical description and need not be given prominence.
Since, in the case of independent works subsequently bound
together, the note may not apply to other copies of the work,
it is generally given as the last note in the entry. For the
second or any succeeding work in the volume, for which the
note may be necessary to identify the work on the shelves or
to explain a call number that appears to be incorrect, a prom-
inent position is desirable.

B. In the case of works issued together in one cover, the note begins:

> Issued with
> Issued with the author's

C. If two or more works are issued together in a case, the note begins:

> Issued in a case with

D. In the case of works issued independently and subsequently bound together, the note begins:

> Bound with
> Bound with the author's

E. The citation of the other work or works in the volume, to be added to the above, takes the following form: the author's name in catalog entry order, forenames represented by initials; brief title (the uniform title, if one is used); place and date of publication; and size if it varies two or more centimeters from the size of the other work. If the work is in a non-Roman script, the bibliographical citation is given in romanization only. If there are more than two works bound together, all of the other works are cited in the entry for the first work in the volume; in the entries for succeeding works only the first work is cited.

> Bound with the author's Observations on the principles which regulate the course of exchange. New York [1969]
> Bound with Jacob, H. Of the sister arts. New York, 1970.
> Bound with Stubbes, G. A dialogue of beauty. New York, 1970. Collins, A. A discourse concerning ridicule and irony in writing. New York, 1970. Oldmixon, J.

Reflections on Dr. Swift's letter to the Earl of
Oxford. New York, 1970.
Issued with Basadre, J. Equivocaciones. Lima,
1928.

F. If the works bound together are numerous (such as a collection of pamphlets or other small works) or are to be classified as a collection, a collective catalog entry is prepared. If the parts are also to be cataloged separately, their place in the collection is indicated. The specification is given in a supplementary note in the analytical entry (see 157).

No. 3 in a vol. with binder's title: Brownist tracts,
1599-1644.
Vol. 140, no. 6, of a collection with binder's title:
Waterman pamphlets.

146. Thesis note

A. General rule. Academic theses presented in partial fulfillment of the requirements for a degree usually carry a formal statement, more or less uniform, depending upon the country of origin, naming the institution or faculty to which the thesis was presented and the degree for which the author was a candidate.[23] This statement is reduced to a brief, formal note giving the designation of the thesis and the institution to which it was presented. The designation of the institution is followed by the date of the degree when

---

23. "Reports" written by candidates for the Ed. D. at Teachers College, Columbia University, are not to be called theses.

it is available from the work being cataloged and varies from the imprint date.

B. Designation of the thesis

1. The English word "thesis" is used to designate all theses. If the author was a candidate for a degree other than that of doctor, this fact is also shown.

> Thesis (M. A.)--Johns Hopkins University.
> Thesis (licenciatura en derecho)--Universidad Nacional Autónoma de México.

Other qualifying terms are added as needed.

> Thesis (thèse complémentaire)--Paris.

2. An abstract, abridgment, summary, or other portion of a thesis is described, as far as possible, by adding to the brief, formal note the qualifying term used in the publication.

> Abstract of thesis--University of Illinois.

C. The degree. Degrees are represented by abbreviations. Authorities for the abbreviations are the catalog of the institution granting the degree and appropriate reference works.[24]

D. The institution. The name of the institution to which the thesis was presented is named as briefly as possible. Most of the older and more famous continental universities

---

24. The Library of Congress uses the latest edition of Webster's new international dictionary and Who's who in America.

are designated simply by the name of the place in which they are located (in the form adopted for author headings in the catalog, omitting the name of the larger geographical entity). For French theses from 1808 to July 10, 1896, the period in which the whole system of French education was centralized as the Université de France with the former universities becoming local faculties, the name of the faculty rather than the university is used in the thesis note.

> Thesis--Yale.
> Thesis--Heidelberg.
> Thesis--Eidgenössische Technische Hochschule.
> Thesis--Faculté de droit de Paris.

E. Edited texts. If the thesis is a text edited by the candidate, and entered under its author or title rather than under the name of the candidate, the thesis note includes the name or designation of the candidate.

> The editor's thesis--University of Chicago.
> Karl Schmidt's thesis--Munich.

F. Joint authors. If the thesis is a work of joint authorship, the thesis note indicates which authors were candidates for degrees.

> The authors' thesis--Johns Hopkins University.
> R. V. Martin's thesis--Ohio State University.

G. Praeses and respondent. In an entry for a foreign thesis in which designation of praeses and respondent is used and the entry is under the praeses (see 12), the name of the respondent (the candidate for the degree) is included in the thesis note.

    Thesis--Wittenberg (P. G. Scheibler, respondent)

    H. Latin theses. If the candidate's name is included in the formal note for a Latin thesis, the surname is given in the form used for the catalog entry and forenames are represented by initials.

    J. Vita. A biographical sketch of the author accompanying his thesis is noted as "Vita" without page citation. If, however, the sketch is printed only on the cover, or on a label mounted on the work, the description is specific.

    Vita: p. [3] of cover.
    Vita on label mounted on last page.

    K. Non-thesis edition

    1. If, in works lacking a formal thesis statement, it is indicated that the publication represents the author's thesis, submitted to a named university, this fact is recorded as a note. The date of the degree is added according to the provisions of 146A.

    Originally presented as the author's thesis, Göttingen.
    Originally presented as the author's thesis, Harvard, 1964.
    Originally presented as the author's thesis (M. A.), Yale.
    Originally presented as the author's thesis, Heidelberg, under the title:

    2. If a copy of an edition without a thesis statement is designated as a thesis by means of a mounted label, or the

addition of a special title page, a formal thesis note is provided. A note is provided to explain the nature of the statement:

> Thesis statement stamped on cover.
> Extra t. p. with thesis statement inserted.

3. In describing works that are revisions of theses or that merely originiated in or are based on theses, it is generally preferable to quote or paraphrase the statement in the work which provides the information.

> A revision of the author's thesis, University of Michigan.

147. "Habilitationsschriften," "Rektoratsreden," "Programmschriften," etc.

A. In cataloging treatises, addresses, and essays presented to European schools or institutions of higher learning as matter of routine or on special occasions, a formal note similar to that used in describing academic theses is generally used. The note is stated in terms of the work as far as possible and gives the following information: the character of the work, the institution to which it was presented, and the occasion of the presentation if the work is not of a routine character.

> Habilitationsschrift--Zurich.
> Rede--Tübingen (Geburtstag des Königs), 1915.

B. If it is issued with a "program" this fact is shown.

> Accompanies "Programm" (Index scholarum sem. aest.)--Greifswald.

Accompanies "program" (Inbjudning till professor-
installation)--Lund.
Separate from "Programm"--Gelehrtenschule des
Johanneums, Hamburg.

C. If, however, the material accompanying the "program" is cataloged as an analytical entry for a serial publication that is entered under the name of the institution, the
"program" note does not repeat the name of the institution.

Universität Tübingen. Bibliothek.
Verzeichniss indischer Handschriften der Königlichen
Universitäts-Bibliothek.

In Universität Tübingen. Tübinger Universitäts-
schriften aus dem Jahr 1865. Tübingen, 1866.
25 cm. 24 p.
Accompanies "Programm" (Geburtsfest des Königs
Karl von Wurttemberg)

148. Contents notes

Preliminary note.

1. Either all of the contents or a part of them are
specified in the catalog entry if it is necessary to bring out
important parts of the work not mentioned in the title and
statement of authorship area, or to give a fuller and more
detailed description of the contents than the title supplies.
If an added entry is to be made for an item in the work,
the presence of this item is specified in the contents or
informal contents note. The complete contents are listed
in the entry for collections of works by the same author
(especially if they are on different subjects) or for collections of works by different authors. If, however, the

articles are numerous (i.e. more than twenty-five items), or slight, or if the collection contains the complete works of an author in one volume, the contents are not listed.

2. Contents are especially necessary for works in several volumes, whether they are single works (with a formal division of matter that can be described) or collections of works by one or more authors.

3. The contents of Festschriften are usually itemized, subject to the limitation on the number of items stated above. Contents are not generally given for composite works unless they fall into the category of Festschriften.

A. Informal contents notes

1. Informal contents notes are used for selected items in a work (generally no more than three) which need to be specified. The following types of items are noted: summaries in languages other than that of the text; bibliographies, discographies, filmographies, and indexes, unless they are obviously of little value; bibliographical references, when they seem to be particularly important or take the place of a bibliography that would have been noted; appendices, if they contain important matter. Supplements, other appended matter, and errata slips not printed as part of the work are always noted (see 155). Other types of items are noted if, in the judgment of the cataloger, their importance warrants noting them.

2. Informal contents notes are given last among the notes unless a formal contents note is also required (see B below); in that case the informal notes precede the formal note. They are generally given in the order of the items in the work, each note forming a separate paragraph.

3. With the exceptions noted below, the specification of each item consists of the precise title of the item as found in the work (generally as a caption or heading of the piece, or in a table of contents) enclosed in quotation marks. The inclusive pagination of each item is specified unless the item is scattered throughout the work. In the latter case a statement phrased by the cataloger is used. The words "Bibliography," "Discography," and "Filmography" (without quotation marks) are preferred to the precise heading found in the work unless the latter is necessary to show the scope of the bibliography, discography, or filmography, or unless the compiler is to be named. Indexes are specified by the conventional note "Includes index [indexes]" (without quotation marks).

Bibliography: p. [221]-[246]
Bibliography: p. 18-25 (3d group)
  (Used when the collation includes more than one group of pages)
Bibliography: v. 1, p. 351-358; v. 2, p. 234-235.
"Chronological list of the author's works": p. 469-475.
"List of works by William Hull": p. 242.
"Analytical digest of treaty provisions, by Herbert A. Smith": p. 159-216.
Includes bibliographies and index.
Appendices (p. 157-200): A. The Anglo-Japanese alliance. --B. The Russo-Japanese peace treaty. --C. The Japan-Korean agreement.

B. Formal contents notes

1. Formal contents notes are used when the entire contents of the work, or several items other than those of the types indicated in A1 above, are to be specified.

2. A formal contents note (because of its length and the fact that in an open entry it will have additions) follows all notes specified above.

3. The items are arranged in one paragraph (for an exception, see 10 and 11 below), beginning with the word "Contents" or the phrase "Partial contents," and are given in the order in which they appear in the work. The specification of each item consists of the title as it is found in the work (generally as a caption or in a table of contents) but without quotation marks. Subtitles and qualifying statements are omitted unless the title is meaningless without them. Introductions recorded in the formalized part of the entry are not mentioned again in the contents paragraph. Prefatory and similar matter is normally omitted.

4. In listing works by different authors, the name of the author, in inverted form if possible, precedes the title, as indicated in the examples below. Initials are used for one or more forenames. The number of names to be included is governed by 134D7; brackets are not used to show that the abbreviation "et al." has been supplied. If an item presents a problem of choice of entry, the cataloger selects

the name which, because of the wording in the source on which the contents note is based, appears to be the name of the principal author instead of attempting to follow the rules in Chapter 1. The designations of function "ed." or "comp." are omitted.

5. In works of one volume, the items in the contents paragraph are separated by a period followed by a dash. Chapter and section numbers are omitted.

6. In works of more than one bibliographical volume, the numbers of the volumes are designated, the terms being those used in the work itself, abbreviated if possible (see Appendix III), except that Arabic numerals are substituted for Roman numerals unless both are required for clarity. If the term is long and there is no standard abbreviation for it, the term is omitted. If the volumes are unnumbered, numbers are supplied in brackets. If the number of bibliographical volumes does not correspond with the number of physical volumes and the collation needs amplification, the number of physical volumes follows the title.

7. For multivolume works, except for the first volume, the dash precedes the volume number; items within the volumes are punctuated as separate sentences.

8. If the volumes of a set are of different editions (see 135E), the edition statements and imprint dates are given in the contents paragraph.

9. Paging is given in the contents paragraph only for a particular item that occupies a disproportionately large portion of the work. If the paging is given, it is cited in parentheses.

10. Contents of a set in many volumes may be paragraphed, one paragraph to a volume, with the word "Contents" centered as a heading.

11. Contents of a collection of separately published pamphlets may be given in tabular form, with the word "Contents" centered as a heading, the author's name given first in inverted form, and the imprint date added after each title. The tabular form is preferred if series numbers are to be specified in the contents (see 142B).

PARTIAL CONTENTS: Baptisms, 1816-1872.--Church members, 1816-1831.--Fellows, L. H. History of the Second Presbyterian Church of West Durham.

CONTENTS: How these records were discovered.--A short sketch of the Talmuds.--Constantine's letter ...

CONTENTS: Brinton, H. H. Introduction.--Whitney, J. William I. Hull, a biographical sketch.--Aydelotte, F. George Fox as a man.

CONTENTS: Irving, W. Rip Van Winkle.--Scott, Sir W. Wandering Willie's tale.--Hawthorne, N. Young Goodman Brown.--Hawthorne, N. Dr. Heidegger's experiment.--Poe, E. A. William Wilson.--Hawthorne, N. The celestial railroad.

CONTENTS: Paula, E. S. de. Tartesso e a rota do estanho.--Gagé, J. Gados, as navegações atlânticas e a rota das Índias na antiguidade.

CONTENTS: Conflict of opinion.--The setting: Deutscher, I. The leader and the party. Erlich, A. The

problem of industrial development. Daniels, R. V.
The struggle with the right opposition. Bauer, R. A.
Ideological revision. --The revolution from above:
Stalin, J. The socialist drive. Nove, A. Economics
and personality. Gordon, M. The fate of the workers.
Lewin, M. Collectivization: the reasons. Fainsod, M.
Collectivization: the method. --The counterrevolution
from above: Dallin, D. J. The return of inequality.
Counts, G. S. The repudiation of experiment. Brown,
E. J. The mobilization of culture. ...

CONTENTS: v. 1. Plain tales from the hills. --
v. 2-3. Soldiers three, and military tales. --v. 4. In
black and white. --v. 5. The phantom 'rickshaw, and
other stories. --v. 6. Under the deodars. The story of
the Gadsbys. Wee Willie Winkie. --v. 7. ...

CONTENTS: t. 1. Dulce y sabrosa. 4. ed. 1921. --
t. 2. La honorada. 3. ed. 1916. --t. 3. ...

CONTENTS: [1] Introduction. --[2] Text.

CONTENTS: Bd. 1. Die logische Theorie des Urteils
bei Aristoteles. Berichtigte Neuausg., mit einem
Anhang: Die Echtheit der aristotelischen Hermeneutik. --
Bd. 2. Die logische Theorie des Syllogismus und die
Entstehung der aristotelischen Logik. 2 v.
(Collation: 2 v. in 3)

CONTENTS
[1] American Peace Society. Should the United States
of America join the Permanent Court of International
Justice? [1931]
[2] Bustamente y Sirvén, A. S. de. The World Court
and the United States. [1929]

CONTENTS
n:o 1. Mertens, R. Die Eidechsen der Kapverden.
(XV, 5 of the series)
n:o 2. Wygodzinsky, P. Thysanura. (XV, 11)

149. International Standard Book Number (ISBN)[25]

A. The International Standard Book Number (ISBN) is

---

25. The Library of Congress will also record the price
for current imprints whenever the information is available;

recorded following the last item in the notes area. It is recorded as found in the publication, preceded by the letters "ISBN. "[26]

    ISBN 0-7131-1646-3

B. In the case of works issued in several volumes, each with its own ISBN, the ISBN is followed by a parenthetical qualifier to indicate the particular volume to which it applies. Multiple ISBN's may follow each other, separated by periods, or they may be recorded on separate lines.

    ISBN 0-8422-7088-6 (v. 1). ISBN 0-8422-7121-X (v. 2)

        or

    ISBN 0-8422-7088-6 (v. 1)
    ISBN 0-8422-7121-X (v. 2)

150. "Title romanized" note[27]

A note giving the romanization of the title is provided for each work the title of which is in non-Roman script unless the romanization has been given preceding the transcription of the title, or unless a uniform title has been used. The note begins with the words "Title romanized, " followed by a colon and the title of the work in romanized form according

------

in certain instances the type of binding will also be recorded.

26. In Library of Congress cataloging the ISBN's will appear whenever possible with proper segmentation indicated by hyphens, separating the country segment, the publisher segment, the work segment, and the check digit.

27. For Library of Congress practice see footnote 2, p. 2.

to the approved system of romanization. If the title is long, only the first part (enough to stand alone) is romanized. If the title contains a numeral or an abbreviation, the word it represents is substituted for it.

151. Tracing

Preliminary note. If required, the catalog entry includes a tracing, or record, of all of the subject entries and added entries (see 33) that are to be made for the work.

A. This tracing is given following the ISBN area. The subject headings are listed first, numbered consecutively with Arabic numerals, followed by the added entry headings numbered with Roman numerals. Added entry headings for persons are given first, followed by those for corporate bodies; within each category the headings are given in the order in which they appear in the entry. Author-title added entry headings are included in the appropriate category. Added entry headings for the title proper, titles other than the title proper, and for series follow in this order.

B. The tracing of the title proper is indicated only by the word "Title." Added entry headings for titles other than the title proper are indicated in full, preceded by the word "Title."

I. Title: Employee manual.

C. When the title of a publication originally issued in a non-Roman script is used as a subject or added entry, it is indicated in romanized form only.

> I. Title. II. Title: Voitel'nit̂sa.
> I. Series: Mekhorah.

D. If the series, or the series in the first set of parentheses if there is more than one, is entered as it appears
in the series area, only the word "Series" is given in the
tracing. Any variation between the series statement and the
series entry is shown.[28] If the series statement includes an
ISSN, the ISSN is omitted from the series entry.

> Statement: (Veröffentlichungen der Schleswig-Holsteini-
> schen Universitäts-Gesellschaft ; Nr. 43)
> Tracing: I. Series: Schleswig-Holsteinische Universi-
> täts-Gesellschaft. Veröffentlichungen der
> Schleswig-Holsteinischen Universitäts
> -Gesellschaft ; Nr. 43.

> Statement: (S. P. E. tract ; no. 36)
> Tracing: I. Series: Society for Pure English. S. P. E.
> tract ; no. 36.

> Statement: (1000 Bilder aus 25 Jahren deutscher Ge-
> schichte ; T. 2)
> Tracing: I. Series: Tausend Bilder aus fünfundzwanzig
> Jahren deutscher Geschichte ; T. 2.

> Statement: (Cahier I. D. E. E. ; no 2)
> Tracing: I. Series: Association pour l'innovation et le
> dynamisme economique dans l'entreprise.
> Cahier I. D. E. E. ; no 2.

E. If a second series (or the first series, if for any
reason it is not given in the customary position following the

---

28. It is necessary to trace the series in full to show
the correct number if an incorrect number appearing in the
work is recorded and corrected in the series statement (e. g.
v. 3 [i. e. 5]) since the added entry is prepared with the
correct number only (e. g. v. 5).

collation) is traced, its catalog entry is always specified.

F. If two or more volumes, or parts of the series, that are not consecutively numbered are included in the series statement, only the first number, followed by "[etc.]," is included in the tracing.

SPECIAL RULES

152. Issues and photoreproductions treated as such

A. The various issues of a given edition may be cataloged as copies, as different issues, or as different editions (see Introductory notes--Identification). Issues treated as copies are noted, with variations being specified.[29] This note is given in a form known as a "dash" entry. It begins with a long dash to represent the repetition of the author heading, followed by a second long dash to represent the repetition of the title. If there is no author heading the note begins with a single long dash.

> ---- ------ Copy 2. Not numbered. Extra-illustrated.
> ---- ------ Copy 2. Bound with ...
> ------ Copy 2. Interleaved, with additions in ms.

B. If variations between issues are so great that the publications cannot be treated as copies but the title and text of the works are the same, they are cataloged as different issues. Dashes, as for copies, are added, followed by the

---

29. The Library of Congress does not note variations in the imprint date nor in the form of name of the publisher.

phrase "Another issue" and the specification of the bibliographical details which differentiate the issue received later
(see also footnote 2, p. 2). Prescribed punctuation is used
when appropriate.

    ---- ------ Another issue.
      30 cm. -- Large paper ed.

    ---- ------ Another issue.
      104 p. (p. 101-104 advertisements)

    ---- ------ Another issue. Calcutta : Asia Pub. House,
    1964.
      (The other issue has imprint: New York : Asia Pub.
      House, 1964)

C. A photoreproduction which is neither a facsimile edition nor a reprint edition is added to the card for the original
work in the same manner as another issue.[30]   Significant
data concerning the reproduction are included (see 156).

    ---- ------ Microfilm. Ann Arbor, Mich. : Univer-
    sity Microfilms, 1968. -- 1 reel ; 35 mm. --
    (American culture series ; 359. 12)

    ---- ------ Micro-opaque. Rochester, N. Y. :
    University of Rochester Press, 1960. -- 3 cards ;
    7. 5 x 12. 5 cm.

    ---- ------ Photocopy. Ann Arbor, Mich. : Univer-
    sity Microfilms, 1965.

153. Offprints

A. An offprint, or separate, of an article, chapter or
other portion of a larger work is cataloged as an independent monograph if the larger work is not in the library's

---

30. The Library of Congress catalogs microform editions
separately.

collections.   The relationship to the larger work is specified.

B. If the larger work is in the library, an analytical
entry is prepared for the part represented by the offprint
and the latter is described with a "dash" entry as explained
in 152B. (See also 157.)

---- ------ Offprint.
   Cover dated 1946.

154. Detached copies of parts of works

A. A part of a work detached from a copy of the work as
a whole, in order to be classified as a separate work or for
some other reason, is cataloged as if it were bibliographically independent; the resulting entry is not an analytical
entry.   An explanatory note is added to the catalog entry.

   Davis, Sir John Francis, bart., 1795-1890.
     Poeseos Sinensis commentarii = On the poetry of the
Chinese / read May 2, 1829 by John Francis Davis. --
[London : s. n., 1830]
     p. 393-461 ; 29 cm.

    Detached from Transactions of the Royal Asiatic
Society of Great Britain and Ireland, v. 2.

B. If, however, the library has a copy of the larger
work as well as the detached copy of the part, an analytical
entry (see 157) is prepared for the part and the detached
copy is noted in the form of a "dash" entry.

---- ------ Detached copy.

155. Supplements, indexes, etc.

Scope. The rules below provide for the description of continuations, supplements, and indexes which, under the provisions of 19A, are to be made part of the cataloging of the works to which they are related.[31]

A. Supplements described in detail

1. Main work entered under author. A long dash to represent the repetition of the author heading and a second long dash to represent the title of the main work are added to the entry following all of the notes relating to the main work, but preceding the tracing. The dashes are followed by the title of the supplement or index, omitting the title of the main work if it is included in the title of the supplement and can be separated from it (see also 3 below); the author statement (if necessary to show the compiler or other person responsible for the supplement or index); the edition statement; imprint; collation; etc. as for an independent work. Prescribed punctuation is used.

> Walpole, Horace, Earl of Orford, 1717-1797.
>   The letters of Horace Walpole, fourth Earl of Orford / chronologically arranged and edited with notes and indices by Mrs. Paget Toynbee. -- Oxford : Clarendon Press, 1903-1905.
>   16 v. : 58 ports. ; 20 cm.

---

31. If the main work is not in the library, a skeleton entry for the main work, to which the description of the dependent part can be added, is prepared. This entry consists of the author and title, or the title, of the main work.

---- ------ Supplement / chronologically arranged
and edited with notes and indices by Paget Toynbee. --
Oxford : Clarendon Press, 1918-1925.
  3 v. : 2 fold. facsims., ports. ; 20 cm.

2. Main work entered under title. If the main work is
entered under title, the provisions of 1 above are followed
except that a single long dash to represent the title of the
main work is used.

  A History of Hampshire and the Isle of Wight. --
  Westminster : Constable, 1900-1912.
    5 v. : ill., facsims., maps, ports. ; 32 cm. --
  (The Victoria history of the counties of England)

    Vols. 3-5 have title : The Victoria history of
    Hampshire and the Isle of Wight.

  ------ Index. -- London : Constable, 1914.
    135 p. ; 32 cm.

3. Title of main work inseparable from title of supplement.
If the title of the main work is grammatically inseparable
from the title of the supplement or if the title of the main
work is included in the title of the supplement in such a
form that it is not readily identified, the provisions of 1
above are followed except that one long dash is used and
the title of the main work is transcribed as part of the title
of the supplement.

  Hungary. Országgyűles. Könyvtár.
    A Képviselőház könyvtárának katalógusa, 1866-
  1893. -- Budapest : Pesti Könyvnyomda, 1894.
    clxi, 881 p.; 24 cm.

  ----A Képviselőházi könyvtár katalógusának
  pótkötete, 1893-1899 / szerk. Küffer Béla. --
  Budapest : Pesti Könyvnyomda, 1899.
    vii, [885]-1457 p. ; 24 cm.

Hansen, Lester Welhaven, 1886-
   The Anderson-Krogh genealogy : ancestral lines and
descendants / compiled by Lester W. Hansen. --
St. Petersburg, Fla. : [s. n.], 1956.
   323 p. : ill., coats of arms, facsims., geneal.
tables ; 23 cm.

   On spine: Anderson-Amundson-von Krogh family.
   Bibliography: p. 146.

---- A supplement to the Anderson-Amundson-von
Krogh family, 1956 edition. -- [St. Petersburg? Fla. :
s. n.], 1971.
   165 p. ; 23 cm.

B. Supplements noted briefly

1. Supplements that are minor in character but that are
not treated according to the provisions of 141F may simply
be noted informally.

   "Tables I, II, and III omitted by error from report"
   published as suppl. (5 p.) and inserted at end.
   "Armorial général de France. Table des noms in-
   scrits dans ce recueil" issued as special suppl. with
   v. 9-14 (1863-69)

2. If contents are given for the main work, the supplementary volumes may be included as part of the contents
statement, even though they are not numbered consecutively
with the other volumes.

   ... v. 10. Southern California. Grand Cañon of the
   Colorado River. Yellowstone National Park.--
   Supplementary volume[s]: [no. 1] Ireland (two lectures)
   Denmark. Sweden. no. 2. Canada (two lectures)
   Malta. Gibraltar.

   ... 5. 1705-1708.--6. 1709-1722.--[7] General
   index.

156. Photoreproductions to be described as such

Preliminary note. Photographic[32] techniques may be used to make a single copy or multiple copies of a work, in microform or in macroform. They may be used as a method of production for original publication, for facsimile editions, or for reprint editions. In some cases the fact that a work is a photoreproduction is of significance for cataloging purposes. This rule provides for cataloging such reproductions.

The use of photographic techniques is ignored for cataloging purposes in the case of reissues by the same publisher, reprint editions, facsimile editions, and original editions in macroform reproduced from copy made or assembled specifically for the purpose of the edition. Such publications are cataloged under the general rules for monographs, serials, music, etc.

Microform reproductions that are not original editions (see 156C) and macroform reproductions not excluded from this rule by the preceding paragraph are described primarily in terms of the photoreproduced original if the description of the original can be determined from the reproduction or from a reliable source. For the description of photoreproductions as issues see 152C.

---

32. "Photographic" is used here to indicate any process of reproduction involving radiant energy.

A. Description of original. The work which is reproduced is described according to the general rules for cataloging monographs, serials, music, etc. The collation, or some part of it, cannot always be determined; it is then necessarily omitted or given as completely as possible.

B. Description of reproduction. The reproduction is described in a note following any notes that pertain to the original. This note incorporates three elements:

1. The general type of reproduction is described by one of the following terms: microfilm, microfiche, micro-opaque, photocopy (or other appropriate term), or, if the type is uncertain, photoreproduction. Negatives are indicated parenthetically.

> Microfilm (negative)
> Photocopy (negative)

When a statement describing the physical form of the original is required, it is included in this note.

> Photocopy of typescript.
> Microfilm (negative) of ms.

2. The organization, firm, or individual responsible for the reproduction, and the place and year in which the reproduction was made are given in conventional imprint order, if readily ascertainable, with prescribed punctuation. For the treatment of more than one agent (i.e. distributor, sponsor, etc.) see 138B. In the case of rare books, the specific copy of the work from which the reproduction was made is identified.

Micro-opaque. Louisville, Ky. : Lost Cause Press, 1957.
Microfilm of the original in the Medina collection,
Biblioteca Nacional de Chile. Providence : Brown University Library, 1941.

3. The physical description of a microreproduction consists of the number of pieces (cards, sheets, reels, containers, etc.) and the size (see 141E). The width of microfilm is given in millimeters; the height and width of sheet microreproductions are given in centimeters.

    2 sheets ; 9 x 12 cm.
    4 cards ; 7. 5 x 12. 5 cm.
    6 boxes of cards ; 25 cm.
    1 reel ; 35 mm.

Shirley, James, 1596-1666.
    The gentleman of Venice : a tragi-comedie presented
at the private house in Salisbury Court by Her Majesties servants / written by James Shirley. -- London :
H. Moseley, 1655.
    78 p. ; 18 cm.

    Micro-opaque. New York : Readex Microprint,
1953. -- 1 card ; 23 x 15 cm. -- (Three centuries of
drama : English, 1642-1700)

The physical description of a macroreproduction is given only
if it differs significantly from the description of the original.

National Civil Liberties Bureau.
    War-time prosecutions and mob violence involving
the rights of free speech, free press, and peaceful
assemblage, from April 1, 1917, to March 1, 1919 /
National Civil Liberties Bureau. -- New York : The
Bureau, 1919.
    55 p. ; 22 cm.
    Photocopy (negative)   55 p. on [28] leaves ; 25 x 30 cm.

Hopp, Ralph Harvey, 1915-
    A study of the problem of complete documentation in
science and technology / by Ralph Harvey Hopp. --

Thesis--University of Illinois.
Vita.
Bibliography: leaves 112-118.
Photocopy of typescript. Ann Arbor, Mich. : University Microfilms, 1958. -- 20 cm.

Prescribed collation punctuation is used in all cases.

C. Original editions in microform. When the copy that is photoreproduced was prepared or assembled specifically for the purpose of bringing out an original edition in microform, the photoreproduction is cataloged according to its own indicia of identification. The physical description (see B3 above) is given in collation position, and the statement of the type of reproduction (see B1 above) is given as the first note. If the photoreproduced work is paged or foliated, the pagination or foliation is given in parentheses following the statement of the number of physical units of the microform.

Baker, C   L
The first six million prime numbers / C. L. Baker and F. J. Gruenberger. -- Madison, Wis. : Published by the Microcard Foundation [for] the RAND Corp., Santa Monica, Calif., 1959.
8 p. ; 23 cm. & 62 cards (7.5 x 12.5 cm.) in pockets.
The cards are micro-opaques.

Regan, Brian T   1938-
The Gothic word / by Brian T. Regan. -- 1st ed. -- Albany : State University of New York Press, 1972.
4 sheets (364 p.) ; 11 x 15 cm.
Microfiche.
Bibliography: p. 364.

157. Analytical entries

Definition and scope. An analytical entry is an entry for a part of a work or series of works for which another, comprehensive, entry is made. The part analyzed may be a complete volume, bibliographically independent from the set of which it forms a part, or it may be a mere page or two which is inadequately described (either from the author or the subject approach) by the catalog entry for the work as a whole. If the part analyzed is an independent work, it is cataloged according to the rules for separately published monographs, with a series statement indicating its relationship to the more comprehensive work. The rules below are limited to analytical entries for parts not bibliographically independent, i. e. parts without numbers to distinguish them from other parts of the more comprehensive work. These entries are commonly called "page" analyticals or "in" analyticals.

A. Parts with special title pages and separate paging

1. If the part to be analyzed has a special title page, the catalog entry through the imprint area is prepared according to the rules for separately published monographs. If it has also separate paging, the form of the collation corresponds also to that for separately published monographs. The first note shows the relationship of the part to the larger work. This "analytical" note begins with the work "In, " printed in boldface or underlined, and contains the following items, in this order: author's name and initials of forenames (for which may be substituted "his, " "her, " "their, " or "its",

printed in boldface or underlined, when the author is the same as that of the part analyzed, brief title, edition, place and date of publication of the larger work.

Colman, Benjamin, 1673-1747.
The hainous nature of the sin of murder, and the great happiness of deliverance from it, as it was represented in a sermon at the lecture in Boston, Sept. 24, 1713, before the execution of one David Wallis / by Benjamin Colman. -- Boston : Printed by J. Allen for N. Boone, 1713.
34 p. ; 14 cm.

<u>In</u> Mather, C. The sad effects of sin. Boston, 1713.

2. If the larger work is in more than one volume, the number of the particular volume analyzed is added after the imprint, followed, in parentheses, by the date of the volume, unless it is the same as that of the larger work. If the larger work is still being published, its imprint dates are omitted.

<u>In</u> Harleian miscellany. London, 1808-1813. v. 3 (1809)

B. Parts with separate title page and continuous paging. The collation of a part paged continuously with other matter in the same volume is omitted. Instead the analytical note contains, in addition to items specified in A1 above, the size of the volume, volume number (if any), inclusive pagination, and important illustrative matter.

Flaminiani,
Ethelinda : an English novel / done from the Italian of Flaminiani. -- London : [J. Watts], 1729.

<u>In</u> Croxall, S., comp. A select collection of novels and histories. 2d ed. London, 1729. 17 cm. v. 5, p. [79]-124.

C. Parts without special title pages. If the part to be analyzed does not have a special title page, the descriptive portion of the entry consists only of the title and statement of authorship area and the edition area if required, followed by the analytical note.

Richardson, Henry Gerald, 1884-
The morrow of the Great charter : an addendum / by H. G. Richardson.

In John Rylands Library. Bulletin of the John Rylands Library, Manchester. Manchester. 27 cm. v. 29 (1945), p. 184-200.

If the part has separate paging only, the total number, as represented by the last numbered page or leaf, is given in the analytical note.

D. Analytical entries for parts of analyzed parts. If an analytical entry is required for a part of a work which is itself cataloged by means of an analytical entry, the analytical note mentions both of the works in which the part is contained, since the information about either may be necessary to locate the work on the shelves and to explain the call number. The lesser work is given first, then the comprehensive work.

In Blümlein, C., comp. Die Floia und andere deutsche maccaronische Gedichte. Strassburg, 1900. (Drucke und Holzschnitte des XV. und XVI. Jahrhunderts in getreuer Nachbildung ; 4)
In The Sacred books of China : the texts of Täoism. Oxford, 1891. 23 cm. v. 1, p. [45]-124. (The Sacred books of the East ; v. 39)

E. Added entries as analytical entries

1. If the catalog entry for a work includes (in title, contents, or other place) reference to a part for which analytical entry is required, an added entry may be made instead of a separate analytical entry.

> Smith, Alfred Emanuel, 1873-1944.
>   Addresses of Alfred E. Smith, delivered at the meetings of the Society of the Friendly Sons of St. Patrick, 1922-1944. ... -- [New York] : Society of the Friendly Sons of St. Patrick in the City of New York, 1945.
>   129 p. : col. facsim., port. ; 24 cm.
>   "Address of Honorable James A. Foley": p. 4-19.
>
> I. Society ... II. Foley, James A., 1882-1946.

2. If the part has been, or is likely to be, published separately or referred to by its title, the added entry takes the form of the author and title of the part.

> Wieland, Christoph Martin, 1733-1813.
>   Der Geist Shakespears / Christoph Martin Wieland. -- Biberach an der Riss : Wege und Gestalten, 1964.
>   p. 184-195 : facsims. ; 19 cm. -- (Wege und Gestalten)
>   "Auszüge aus dem Hamlet": p. 188-194.
>
> I. Shakespeare, William, 1564-1616. Hamlet. or
> I. Shakespeare, William, 1564-1616. Hamlet. German.
> Selections. II. Title.

3. If, however, the added entries would be so numerous that the tracing would be cumbersome, analytical entries are preferred. Likewise, if the part to be analyzed requires its own secondary entries other than title, such as subject headings, name of translator, etc., the special analytical entries may be necessary.

GLOSSARY

ADDITIONS AND REVISIONS

Added title page.   A title page preceding or following the title page chosen as the basis for the description of the publication. It may be more general, as a series title page, or equally general, as a title page in another language.   In the case of a facsimile edition or a reprint edition with a new title page, a reproduction of the original title page is not treated as an added title page.

Area. A major section of a catalog entry, e. g. the imprint area.

Element.   A sub-section of an area of the catalog entry, e. g. a parallel title.

Facsimile edition. Revise the definition as follows:

Facsimile edition.   An edition which not only provides an exact replica of the text of the work reproduced, but which has as its chief purpose to simulate the physical appearance of the original work.

Graph. A pictorial representation of numerical data, e. g. a bar graph, a broken line graph, a circular graph, a pictogram.

Monograph.   A work or a collection, regardless of format, that is not a serial.

Other title. A title other than the title proper or a parallel title appearing in the publication, e. g. an alternative title, a subtitle.

Other title information. Phrases, other than titles, a statement of authorship, or an edition statement, appearing on the title page, in the preliminaries, or in the colophon and indicative of the character, contents, etc. of the publication, or the motive for, or occasion of, its publication.

Parallel title. The title proper in another language or in another script.

Plate. A leaf containing illustrative matter, with or without text, that does not form a part of the numeration of the pages or leaves of text. It is not an integral part of a gathering. Plates may be distributed throughout the publication or gathered together; they may be numbered or unnumbered. A plate is usually, though not always, made of a different type of paper from that used in the rest of the publication.

Preliminaries. The half title, the added title page, the verso of the title page, the cover, and the spine.

Subseries. A series whose title is indistinctive and is dependent on the title of another series.

Title. Revision of definition of "Title": change the period at the end of the last sentence to a semicolon; add the words: "the title proper." Add as the second and third items of the "See also," "other title," "parallel title."

Title proper. <u>See</u> Title 2.

Appendix III

ABBREVIATIONS

ADDITIONS AND REVISIONS

dissertation delete entry

frontispiece, -s delete entry

illustration, -s change abbreviation to "ill. "

illustrator change abbreviation to "ill. "

inaugural dissertation delete entry

leaf, leaves delete entry and accompanying footnote.

no date (of publication) delete entry

no place of publication change abbreviation to "s. l. [i. e.
  sine loco]"

Add new entries:

   no publisher s. n. [i. e. sine nomine]

   sine loco s. l.

   sine nomine s. n.

Revise footnote 2, p. 358, to read:

   2. Used only in uniform titles in listing languages or
musical instruments and in the collation area to separate
the statement of size from the statement of accompanying
material.

Appendix V

PUNCTUATION AND DIACRITICS

A. Punctuation.

Each area of the catalog entry and the individual elements of each area are separated by the punctuation marks prescribed by the International Standard Bibliographic Description. See 131 for the general rule; details are given in the appropriate rules in Chapter 6.

Within the limitation specified in 131 other punctuation is used as necessary. With few exceptions standard practice is followed. In recording titles and quoted matter in notes, current usage of the language concerned is followed. For special practices with respect to contents notes and analytical notes see the rules and examples in Chapter 6; see also 163, serials holdings.

The following specific practices, in addition to those provided for in the prescribed punctuation, are observed:

Brackets. Brackets are used to enclose the name of a personal or corporate author in the main entry heading if the author's name or pseudonym does not appear in the publication or appears in such a concealed manner that ascription of authorship is not obvious. Titles of nobility, rank, honor, or office are included within the brackets, but not dates or approximate dates of birth and death. Parts of names that do not appear on the publication (e. g.

forenames, or forenames of which only the initials are given) are not enclosed in brackets.

Brackets are not used in the tracing even though the corresponding words are so enclosed in the entry.

Comma. A comma is normally used

1) To separate the surname or family name and the forename or given name, even though it is the normal order in certain countries to give the surname first. See "Entry of name. Introductory notes. 1," p. 80-81 for an exception.

2) To separate date, number, place, or designation from the name or heading, whether personal or corporate, unless a specific rule provides or indicates otherwise.

Parentheses. Parentheses are used in headings for corporate bodies and uniform titles to enclose certain additions supplied by a cataloger for the purpose of definition or identification.

Period. A period is used or omitted after abbreviations and contractions in accordance with current usage of the language concerned. Periods are supplied in the case of certain references from acronyms. They are not supplied after ellipses represented by three dots.

Other usage of periods in catalog entries is best derived from the examples appearing under the rules.

Question mark. The question mark is used to indicate that

the preceding supplied place name or date in an imprint, or date in a heading, is uncertain.

Quotation marks. The special quotation marks used in works in certain foreign languages (e. g. German) are represented by the marks customarily used in English works, except when they enclose words in a script other than the Roman and Cyrillic alphabets.

B. Diacritics

Diacritics are transcribed as found or as provided in tables of romanization. When absent, they are added in conformity with general usage. They are not added, however, in the body of the entry or in quoted notes for French books published before 1800 or for Spanish books published before 1890.

For the treatment of diacritics in headings for personal names, see 45.

CONCORDANCE OF RULE NUMBERS

1967 Ed.	1974 Ed.	1967 Ed.	1974 Ed.	1967 Ed.	1974 Ed.
130	130	135B	135E	140D	----
131	132	136	135G	141	139
132	133	137	135F	141A	139A
132A4	133A5	138	136	141B	139B
133	134	138A	136A	141C	139C
133A	134B1	138B	136C	141D	139D
133B	134B2	138C	140	141E	139E
133C	134C1	138D	136A	141F	139F
133D	134C3	138E	136F	141G	139G
133E	134B4	138F	136E	141H	139A
133F	134B5	138G	136 D	141J	139H
133G	134C4a	139	137	141K	----
133H	134C4b	139A	137A	142	141
134	134D	139B	----	142A	141B
134A	134D1	139C	137B	142A1	141B1
134B	134D1	139D	137C	142A2	141B2
134C	----	139E	137D	142A3	141B3
134D	134D7	140	138	142A4	141B4
134E	134D8	140A	138A	142A5	141B5
134F	134D9	140B	138B	142A6	141B6
135A	135A, C	140C	138C	142A7	141B7

1967 Ed.	1974 Ed.	1967 Ed.	1974 Ed.	1967 Ed.	1974 Ed.
142A8	141B8	142D	141E	144E	143D
142A9	141B9	142D1	141E1	145	144
142A10	141B10	142D2	141E2	146A-B, D	145A-D
142A11	141B12	142D3	141E3	146C	145E
142B	141C	142D4	141E4	146E	145F
142B1	141C1	142D5	141E5	147	146
142B2	141C2	142E	141F	148	147
142B3	141B3c	142E1	141F2	149	148
142B4	141C4	142E2	141F3	150	150
142B5	141C5	142F	141F2	151	151
142C	141D	143A	142A	151B	151C
142C1	141D1	143B	142B	151C	151D
142C1a	141D1a	143C	142C	151D	151E-F
142C1b	- - - -	143D	142D	152	152
142C2	141D2	143E	142E	153	153
142C3	141D3	143F	142F	154	154
142C4	141D4	144A	143A	155	155
142C5	141D5	144B	143B1	156	157
142C6	141D6	144C	143B2	190-191	156
142C7	141D7	144D	143C		